I0050553

FINANCIAL DIGITALIZATION AND ITS IMPLICATIONS FOR ASEAN+3 REGIONAL FINANCIAL STABILITY

JANUARY 2023

ASIAN DEVELOPMENT BANK

ADB

Creative Commons Attribution 3.0 IGO license (CC BY 3.0 IGO)

© 2023 Asian Development Bank
6 ADB Avenue, Mandaluyong City, 1550 Metro Manila, Philippines
Tel +63 2 8632 4444; Fax +63 2 8636 2444
www.adb.org

Some rights reserved. Published in 2023.

ISBN 978-92-9270-010-2 (print); 978-92-9270-011-9 (electronic); 978-92-9270-012-6 (ebook)
Publication Stock No. TCS230020-2
DOI: http://dx.doi.org/10.22617/TCS230020-2

The views expressed in this publication are those of the authors and do not necessarily reflect the views and policies of the Asian Development Bank (ADB) or its Board of Governors or the governments they represent.

ADB does not guarantee the accuracy of the data included in this publication and accepts no responsibility for any consequence of their use. The mention of specific companies or products of manufacturers does not imply that they are endorsed or recommended by ADB in preference to others of a similar nature that are not mentioned.

By making any designation of or reference to a particular territory or geographic area, or by using the term "country" in this publication, ADB does not intend to make any judgments as to the legal or other status of any territory or area.

This work is available under the Creative Commons Attribution 3.0 IGO license (CC BY 3.0 IGO) https://creativecommons.org/licenses/by/3.0/igo/. By using the content of this publication, you agree to be bound by the terms of this license. For attribution, translations, adaptations, and permissions, please read the provisions and terms of use at https://www.adb.org/terms-use#openaccess.

This CC license does not apply to non-ADB copyright materials in this publication. If the material is attributed to another source, please contact the copyright owner or publisher of that source for permission to reproduce it. ADB cannot be held liable for any claims that arise as a result of your use of the material.

Please contact pubsmarketing@adb.org if you have questions or comments with respect to content, or if you wish to obtain copyright permission for your intended use that does not fall within these terms, or for permission to use the ADB logo.

Corrigenda to ADB publications may be found at http://www.adb.org/publications/corrigenda.

Notes:
ADB recognizes "China" as the People's Republic of China; "Hong Kong" as Hong Kong, China; and "Korea" as the Republic of Korea.

Cover design by Edith Creus.

CONTENTS

TABLES, FIGURES, AND BOXES

ACKNOWLEDGMENTS

This report was written by Shinobu Nakagawa, professor, Faculty of Economics, Saitama University of Japan; Satoru Yamadera, advisor, Economic Research and Regional Cooperation Department of the Asian Development Bank (ADB); Jungwoon Lee, financial sector specialist, Economic Research and Regional Cooperation Department, ADB; and Takeshi Osada, professor, Faculty of Economics, Saitama University of Japan.

The authors would like to thank selected graduate and postdoctoral students of the Saitama School of Economics and Management: Taku Kinai, Toshihiko Okano, Akira Sakai, Yushi Shinada, and Kota Yasumura for their extensive research assistance. The authors also wish to thank ADB consultants Kevin Donahue, Yvonne Osonia, Sheila Sombillo, and Margarita T. Tirona for their editorial review and administrative support.

Lastly, no part of this report represents the official views or opinions of ADB. The authors bear sole responsibility for the contents of this report.

ABBREVIATIONS

ACPR	Autorité de contrôle prudentiel et de resolution (French Prudential Supervision and Resolution Authority)
ADB	Asian Development Bank
ADBI	Asian Development Bank Institute
ADGM	Abu Dhabi Global Markets
AE	advanced economies
AFM	Netherlands Authority for the Financial Markets
AMF	Autorité des marchés financiers
AMS	ASEAN member states
APAC	Asia-Pacific
API	application programming interfaces
AI	artificial intelligence
AML	anti-money laundering
APN	Asian Payment Network
ASEAN	Association of Southeast Asian Nations
ASEAN+3	Association of Southeast Asian Nations (ASEAN) and the People's Republic of China (PRC), Japan, and the Republic of Korea
ASIC	The Australian Securities and Investments Commission
AUM	assets under management
B2B	business-to-business
BaFin	The Federal Financial Supervisory Authority
BCBS	Basel Committee on Banking Supervision
BDF	Banque de France
BIS	Bank for International Settlement
BNPL	buy now/pay later
BoE	Bank of England
BOJ	Bank of Japan
C2B	consumer-to-business
C2C	consumer-to-consumer
CBN	correspondent banking network
CCAF	Cambridge Centre for Alternative Finance
CFT	Combating the Financing of Terrorism Compliance
CMIM	Chiang Mai Initiative Multilateralisation
CMG	Crisis Management Group
COVID-19	coronavirus disease
CPMI	Committee on Payments and Market Infrastructures

CRD	Capital Requirements Directive
CSSF	Commission de Surveillance du Secteur Financier
DLT	distributed ledger technology
DNB	De Nederlandsche Bank
ECB	European Central Bank
EBA	European Banking Authority
EEA	European Economic Area
EME	emerging market economies
EMEA	Europe, the Middle East and Africa
EU	European Union
FATF	Financial Action Task Force
FCA	Financial Conduct Authority
FinTech	financial technology
FSA	Financial Services Agency
FSA (Poland)	Financial Supervision Authority
FSC	Financial Services Commission
FSF	Financial Stability Forum
FSB	Financial Stability Board
FSI	Financial Stability Institute
FSMA	Financial Services and Markets Authority
G20	Group of Twenty (Argentina; Australia; Brazil; Canada; People's Republic of China; Germany; France; India; Indonesia; Italy; Japan; Mexico; the Republic of Korea; the Russian Federation; Saudi Arabia; South Africa; Türkiye; the United Kingdom; the United States; and the European Union)
G-SIFIs	global systematically important financial institutions
GFC	global financial crisis
HKMA	Hong Kong Monetary Authority
IAIS	International Association of Insurance Supervisors
ICT	information and communications technology
IMF	International Monetary Fund
INTERPOL	International Criminal Police Organization
IoT	Internet of Things
IT	information technology
IOSCO	International Organization of Securities Commissions
ISO	International Organization for Standardization
KPMG	Klynveld Peat Marwick Goerdeler International Limited
KYC	know your customer
KYCC	know your customer's customer
LEI	legal entity identifiers
LOLR	lender of last resort
MAS	Monetary Authority of Singapore
MiFID	Markets in Financial Instruments Directive
ML	machine learning
MTO	money transfer operator
NBB	National Bank of Belguim

OTC	over-the-counter
P2P	peer-to-peer
POS	point-of-sale
PSD	Payments Services Directive
RegTech	regulatory technology
RPA	Robotic Process Automation
RRP	recovery and resolution plan
RT-RPS	real-time retail payment system
SFC	Securities and Futures Commission of Hong Kong
SMEs	small to medium-sized enterprises
SSM	single supervisory mechanism
SupTech	supervisory technology
TechFin	technology companies, who have been providing software solutions that are not primarily finance-related, and now seek to launch financial services
TC68	ISO Technical Committee 68
TLAC	total loss-absorbing capacity
UK	United Kingdom
USD	United States dollar
WEF	World Economic Forum

EXECUTIVE SUMMARY

This report aims to examine the impact of digitalization on the financial stability of the Association of Southeast Asian Nations (ASEAN) plus the People's Republic of China (PRC), Japan, and the Republic of Korea—a grouping collectively known as ASEAN+3. Dramatic changes have been observed in the region and this report reexamines the impact of these changes on financial regulations. In addition, the report proposes necessary risk mitigation measures along with the transformation of the regional financial landscape since the economic and financial linkages among individual ASEAN+3 markets are becoming much stronger amid the increase of intraregional trade and financial transactions.

The use of digital banking has grown significantly across the globe, mainly due to high rates of internet penetration, widely adopted mobile devices, and increasing customer demand for digital financial services. In select economies in Asia and the Pacific, the digital-banking penetration rate approached 90% in 2021.[1] Across the region, digital wallets have taken hold as the dominant e-commerce payment instrument, accounting for 68% of regional e-commerce transactions value in 2021, which is projected to expand to over 72% by 2025 with the declining use of cash.[2]

The report also highlights recent notable developments and trends in the financial landscape in the advancement of digital technologies, such as the decreasing number of traditional bank branches and ATMs in many high- and middle-income economies; gradual shifting to mobile-based deposit services; emergence of digital bank lending and cross-border digital remittances; and increased use of robotic advisors in asset management, sales, and consulting. The PRC is known to be the most advanced market in terms of personal data usage. The Republic of Korea made a big shift to cashless in early 2000. Previously, such transformations might propagate gradually. However, among the many impacts of the coronavirus disease (COVID-19) pandemic are the acceleration of digital transformation and the removal of barriers to digitalization. Furthermore, ASEAN markets are quickly catching up with the regional leaders.

Digitalization is leading to the unbundling of bank businesses and their transformation across ASEAN+3. In some cases, new firms with advanced technologies have emerged to provide less costly banking services, while existing banks are trying to improve their operations by utilizing information technologies. In other cases, banks have flexibly and effectively outsourced some traditional operations to improve

---

[1] McKinsey & Company's 2021 personal financial services survey covered eight markets in emerging Asia (the People's Republic of China, India, Indonesia, Malaysia, the Philippines, Sri Lanka, Thailand, and Viet Nam) and seven markets in developed Asia (Australia; Hong Kong, China; Japan; the Republic of Korea; New Zealand; Singapore; and Taipei,China).S. Barquin et al. 2021. Emerging Markets Leap Forward in Digital Banking Innovation and Adoption. *McKinsey & Company*. 23 September. https://www.mckinsey.com/industries/financial-services/our-insights/emerging-markets-leap-forward-in-digital-banking-innovation-and-adoption.

[2] For example, Alipay and WeChat Pay are the services in the People's Republic of China. GCash is the service in the Philippines.

their overall business. The former are often called "TechFin" and the latter "FinTech," although there is no clear definition of either term. Nonetheless, new technologies continue to transform the banking industry and increase competition within it as well as with different industries.

Financial digitalization further promotes cross-border banking activities. The concept of jurisdictional border and physical presence, such as branches and subsidiaries, may become unclear from a mid- to long-term perspective. As economic linkages among ASEAN+3 economies are strong, cross-border banking and offerings of various financial services are expected to increase and change ASEAN+3's financial landscape. Cross-border banking will no longer be a privileged service provided by big banks. As the sunk cost of cross-border operation declines, it can be provided by various service providers. Given an enabling environment and the advantage of digital banks, even cross-border branchless banking might emerge in the future. Such transformation will bring benefits, but it is also important to bear in mind the potential risks associated with cross-border banking and digital financial services because there is a gap in supervisory jurisdictions, in which there might be unnecessary overlaps as well as a vacuum of regulations.

This report examines how banks should be regulated and supervised in the digital era. First of all, it emphasizes that the progress of financial digitalization is a great opportunity for the financial industry as a whole. While being aware of the risks involved, technological innovation in financial services should not be fundamentally impeded, and a free and competitive environment should be sufficiently ensured. In this regard, the report reviews the lessons of financial regulatory and supervisory reforms learned from the global financial crisis in the late 2000s, refers to the ongoing efforts being made by global authorities toward financial digitalization, and then identifies the changes in regulations and supervision needed to successfully transform the traditional banking model. Regulations and supervision in the new digital era should be consistent as much as possible with those of the global financial community to avoid creating arbitrage opportunities for banking services.

The measures to be considered in the ASEAN+3 region include (i) ensuring a level-playing field between existing banks and new entrants; (ii) not granting special treatment in bank licensing standards; (iii) eschewing excessive regulations and supervision; (iv) maintaining the existing entity-based framework in principle, flexibly and appropriately applying activity- or risk-based regulations and supervision depending on the type of banking service and the extent of influence on financial system and infrastructure; (v) enhancing regulatory and supervisory coordination and cooperation, particularly between home and host authorities; and (vi) adopting and effectively utilizing so-called regulatory technology, or "RegTech," for reducing the regulatory burden of private financial institutions and supervisory technology, and "SupTech," for improving the capacity of information-sharing among relevant regulators and supervisors. As cybersecurity risks evolve and intensify almost every day and everywhere, further coordination among financial authorities is indispensable, particularly in terms of cross-border data exchanges and standardization.

Then, the report indicates the risk associated with financial integration in the digital era. It is necessary to understand that cyberspace makes the conflict between jurisdictions more complicated. Questions will increase about who should regulate and how, since it is difficult to set a clear national border in cyberspace. At least for the short-term, banking regulations must be applied and governed based on territoriality. Therefore, the principles for the home and host supervisory arrangement continue to remain an important guiding principle for the expansion of cross-border digital financial services. Within ASEAN+3, various levels and scopes of supervisory colleges should be established to enhance cross-border cooperation and information exchange.

The expansion of cross-border banking activities will create more difficulty for supervision and crisis management. Mismanagement of liquidity can trigger a failure of a banking group regionally. The home supervisor can provide liquidity to support the settlement of its own currency, but it is not possible to stop the chain reaction of failures in other markets. Therefore, additional liquidity measures in different local currencies may need to be considered along with the expansion of cross-border financial services, depending on their size, impact on payment and settlement systems, and impact on regional financial stability.

As a regional financial safety net, ASEAN+3 established the Chiang Mai Initiative Multilateralization in 2010. However, it was designed to address the temporary liquidity shortage of a government, not to be acting as the lender of last resort of foreign currency for a particular financial institution. Thus, home and host central banks must prepare their own cross-border short-term liquidity measures, such as cross-border collateral arrangements and bilateral swap agreements, as additional layers of the regional financial safety net.

Cross-border collateral arrangements recognize the home country's government bonds as eligible collateral; thus, by pledging the home country's government bonds to the host central bank, the host central bank can extend a loan to a troubled foreign bank branch. It would prevent a temporary liquidity shortage from developing into default and ensure repayment of temporary liquidity to the host central bank. It would require enhancement of cross-border market infrastructure: desirably, system linkages of domestic market infrastructures.[3]

A bilateral swap agreement can provide the local currency of the host regulator based on the home country's currency. The local currency swap lines between ASEAN+3 central banks can alleviate some market stress in the region because a large portion of intraregional transactions are denominated in United States dollars that are eventually exchanged for local currencies. However, the region's central banks need to pay attention to the risk of moral hazard because the home central bank will take a risk on behalf of an illiquid bank.

Financial regulations and risk mitigation measures must transform along with the digital transformation of financial services. ASEAN+3 is unique compared with other parts of the world. Intraregional economic linkages are extensive, as in the European Union. But member economies have their own currencies, and they are in different stages of economic development, though these differences can be narrowed rapidly. The region is a global leader in the transformation of digital financial services; hence, the opportunities as well as risks involved may be high. Therefore, it is important to consider regional risk mitigation measures along with the rapid expansion of new financial services in ASEAN+3 before any crisis happens.

---

[3] The Cross-Border Settlement Infrastructure Forum under the Asian Bond Markets Initiative has proposed central securities depository–real-tie gross settlement linkages to promote the use of cross-border collateral. Recommendations and proposals are described in ADB. 2020. *Next Steps for ASEAN+3 Central Securities Depository and Real-Time Gross Settlement Linkages*. Manila.

INTRODUCTION | 1

The coronavirus disease (COVID-19) has impacted the social, economic, and financial landscape of Asia. The pandemic has accelerated digitalization, which otherwise would not have been achieved in such a short time. Empirical findings from the Asian Development Outlook 2021 show that countries with better information communication technology infrastructure have been more successful in cushioning the economic shock of the COVID-19 pandemic by shifting more economic activity online.[1] Thus, it is reasonable to conclude that recovery from the pandemic will accelerate digitalization and digital transformation.

The emergence of financial technology (FinTech) start-ups has progressed at an unprecedented pace. According to the Cambridge Centre for Alternative Finance, the Asian Development Bank Institute, and FinTechSpace (2019), more than USD485 million was invested across 68 deals for FinTech start-ups in 2018, which represented 143% year-on-year growth from 2017. The pace of financial digital transformation has been particularly fast in members of the Association of Southeast Asian Nations (ASEAN) plus the People's Republic of China (PRC), Japan, and the Republic of Korea—a grouping that is collectively known as ASEAN+3. The region is becoming one of the world's most advanced markets in which to showcase frontier technologies and applications.

Rapid growth in FinTech is expected to change the financial landscape in ASEAN+3; hence, adjustments to financial regulations will be required. Therefore, it is necessary to take stock of recent discussions on FinTech and related regulations and to consider the potential impacts and necessary changes to financial regulations and the regulatory framework.

It is also necessary to consider the possible implications for cross-border financial regulations. Emerging technologies and the close economic linkages among ASEAN+3 economies can facilitate the cross-border offering of various financial services. The location of financial service providers may become less important, if not irrelevant, while the regulatory framework such providers operate under will continue to be based on geographic boundaries. Since ASEAN+3 has strong intraregional economic interconnectedness similar to the European Union, its potential impact should not be dismissed. It may be necessary to consider possible conflicts of jurisdiction and risk mitigation measures to prevent any financial market disruption resulting from increased cross-border banking and digital financial services.

The outline of this publication is as follows. Section 2 reviews the current ASEAN+3 financial landscape and the impact of digitalization on financial institutions. The section aims to provide a comprehensive

---

[1] Asian Development Bank. 2021. *Asian Development Outlook 2021: Financing a Green and Inclusive Recovery*. Manila. https://www.adb.org/publications/asian-development-outlook-2021.

background and the current status of FinTech developments and future trends. Section 3 reviews banking regulations and supervision in the digital era. The section provides a review of emerging regulatory changes, digitalization, and the digital transformation of traditional banking models and financial services. Section 4 explains risk mitigation measures for more digitally integrated regional financial markets. It emphasizes the importance of cooperation between home and host authorities, particularly in the context of risk mitigation. It also proposes additional regional financial safety nets, such as cross-border collateral and swap agreements among ASEAN+3 central banks, along with the expansion of cross-border digital financial transformation. Section 5 concludes.

REVIEW OF THE DIGITAL FINANCE LANDSCAPE AND THE IMPACT OF DIGITALIZATION ON FINANCIAL INSTITUTIONS

2

Digitalization has made a significant impact on the financial industry worldwide amid a rapidly changing landscape. While technological developments have facilitated the unbundling and transformation of existing financial services, it has also provided opportunities for new firms with digital advantages to enter into financial industries by offering convenient, affordable, and more tailored financial services. To this end, incumbent financial institutions are facing more competition and trying to improve their business efficiency, including through digital transformation. In addition, emerging digital financial services are expanding beyond borders to an unprecedented degree, albeit with additional complications. This section reviews the international landscape of digital finance and its impacts on financial institutions.

Recent Developments in Digital Finance

Digital Banking and Traditional Channels (Bank Branches and ATMs)

The use of digital banking has grown significantly across the globe mainly due to high rates of internet penetration, the widely adopted use of mobile devices, and increasing customer demand for digital financial services. In 2020, there were 1.9 billion users of digital financial services, with this number forecast to reach 2.5 billion by 2024.[2] Digital channels are now used more frequently than bank branches and ATMs.[3] In select jurisdictions of Asia and the Pacific, the digital-banking penetration rate is approaching 90% in 2021.[4] Between 2017 and 2021 in select emerging markets of Asia and the Pacific, the share of consumers actively using digital banking increased sharply, rising from 54% to 88% during the review period. On the other hand, the density of bank branches and ATMs has declined in many countries in response to cost-cutting pressures and customers' shift to digital channels for routine transactions such as bills payment. According to the Committee on Payments and Market Infrastructures (CPMI), the number of bank branches per 1 million people declined by about 13% in from 2012 to 2019 across CPMI jurisdictions, while a similar decline was seen in the total number

---

[2]   Statista. Number of Active Online Banking Users Worldwide in 2020 with Forecasts from 2021 to 2024, by Region. https://www.statista.com/statistics/1228757/online-banking-users-worldwide/ (accessed 12 September 2022).

[3]   V. Srinivas and A. Ross. 2018. Accelerating Digital Transformation in Banking: Findings from the Global Consumer Survey on Digital Banking. *Deloitte Insights*. 9 October. https://www2.deloitte.com/us/en/insights/industry/financial-services/digital-transformation-in-banking-global-customer-survey.html.

[4]   McKinsey's 2021 Personal Financial Services Survey covers eight markets in emerging Asia and the Pacific (the People's Republic of China, India, Indonesia, Malaysia, the Philippines, Sri Lanka, Thailand, and Viet Nam) and seven markets in developed Asia and the Pacific (Australia; Hong Kong, China; Japan; the Republic of Korea; New Zealand; Singapore; and Taipei,China). S. Barquin et al. 2021. Emerging Markets Leap Forward in Digital Banking Innovation and Adoption. *McKinsey & Company*. 23 September. https://www.mckinsey.com/industries/financial-services/our-insights/emerging-markets-leap-forward-in-digital-banking-innovation-and-adoption.

of ATMs per 1 million people in CPMI advanced economies during the same period (**Figure 2.1**).[5] In addition, Forbes reported that the number of bank branches in the United States (US) dropped from 85,993 to 81,586 between 2017 and 2020, a 5.1% decline, due to the move toward expanded digital financial services and a desire to cut costs—this number could fall further to 40,000 by 2027 and then plunge to as low as 16,000 by 2030.[6] In the United Kingdom (UK), more than 4,000 bank branches have closed since 2015 as lenders increase digital financial services for customers.[7] This trend has also been observed in some Asian countries in recent years including Indonesia, Malaysia, the Republic of Korea, Singapore, and Thailand.[8]

Figure 2.1: Number of Bank Branches and Automated Teller Machines per Million Inhabitants in Committee on Payments and Market Infrastructures Jurisdictions

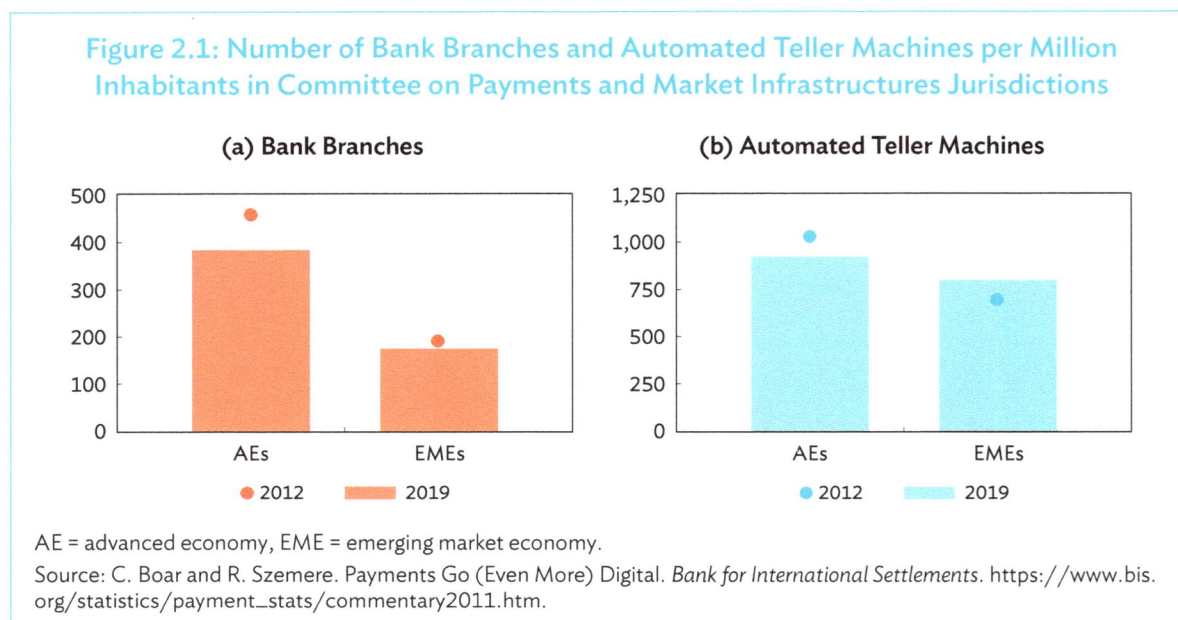

(a) Bank Branches

(b) Automated Teller Machines

● 2012 ▇ 2019

AE = advanced economy, EME = emerging market economy.
Source: C. Boar and R. Szemere. Payments Go (Even More) Digital. *Bank for International Settlements*. https://www.bis.org/statistics/payment_stats/commentary2011.htm.

Digital Payment

The digital innovation is reshaping payments. Consumers are increasingly shifting from physical to digital instruments while digital technologies enable consumers to use efficient, faster, and more convenient payment instruments. From 2012 to 2019, more than half of the member jurisdictions of the CPMI experienced a decline in the use of physical payment means, including cash and cheques, along with a rise in the use of digital payments such as direct debits, credit transfers, contactless cards, and e-money payments (**Figure 2.2**). The average number of digital payments in CPMI jurisdictions

[5] C. Boar and R. Szemere. Payments Go (Even More) Digital. *Bank for International Settlements (BIS)*. https://www.bis.org/statistics/payment_stats/commentary2011.htm.

[6] P. Ghosh. 2021. 3 Major Banks Plan More Branch Closings As Thousands Shutter—In U.S. And U.K.—Amid Covid, Digital Growth. *Forbes*. 23 April. https://www.forbes.com/sites/palashghosh/2021/04/23/3-major-banks-plan-more-branch-closings-as-thousands-shutter-in-us-and-uk-amid-covid-digital-growth/?sh=17276f465bc6.

[7] *Which? Money*. 2022. Bank Branch Closures: Is Your Local Bank Closing? October. https://www.which.co.uk/money/banking/switching-your-bank/bank-branch-closures-is-your-local-bank-closing-a28n44c8z0h5#headline_6.

[8] World Bank. Data. Commercial Bank Branches (Per 100,000 Adults) - Indonesia, Malaysia, Korea, Rep., Singapore, Thailand. https://data.worldbank.org/indicator/FB.CBK.BRCH.P5?locations=ID-MY-KR-SG-TH and https://data.worldbank.org/indicator/FB.ATM.TOTL.P5?locations=ID-MY-KR-SG-TH (accessed 12 September 2022).

Figure 2.2: Payments Are Shifting to Digital Instruments

Number per inhabitant

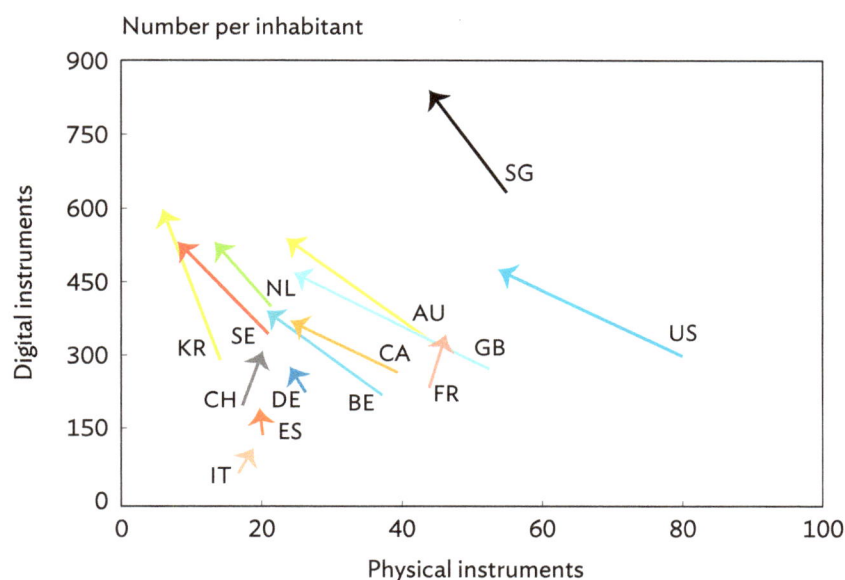

AU = Australia, BE = Belgium, CA = Canada, CH = Switzerland, DE = Germany, ES = Spain, FR = France,
GB = United Kingdom, IT = Italy, KR = Republic of Korea, NL = Netherlands, SE = Sweden, SG = Singapore,
US = United States.

Notes: The start (end) of an arrow represents 2012 (2019). Digital instruments include credit transfers, direct debits, card and e-money payments, and other cashless instruments. Physical instruments include paper-based payment instruments (cheques) and cash withdrawals at ATMs (used as a proxy for cash payments). For Canada, the latest data for cash withdrawals at ATMs are for 2017. For Spain, the start of the arrow represents 2014. For Switzerland and the United Kingdom, physical instruments include cheques and total cash withdrawals.

Source: C. Boar and R. Szemere. Payments Go (Even More) Digital. *Bank for International Settlements*. https://www.bis.org/statistics/payment_stats/commentary2011.htm.

increased by 72% from 176 per inhabitant in 2012 to 303 per inhabitant in 2019. As fast payment systems are rolled out in more CPMI jurisdictions, the number of fast payment transactions per person continues to increase. From 2012 to 2019, payments with contactless cards and online payments were used more frequently. For example, residents in CPMI jurisdictions made 65 contactless card transactions per person on average in 2019, which is about three times more than in 2017. According to the *Global Payments Report* (2022), digital wallets were the most used payment method globally in 2021 (**Figure 2.3**).[9] In e-commerce, digital wallets accounted for 48.6% of global e-commerce transaction value in 2021, followed by credit cards (21%), debit cards (13%), buy now/pay later (3%), and cash (3%). In addition, digital wallets comprised 28.6% of point-of-sale transaction values, followed by credit cards (24%), debit cards (23%), and cash (18%). In Asia and the Pacific, digital wallets—which include Alipay, WeChat Pay, GCash, GrabPay, Pay Pay, and OVO—took hold as the dominant e-commerce payment instrument, accounting for 68.5% of regional e-commerce transaction values in 2021 (**Box 2**); this is projected to expand to over 72% in 2025 with the declining use of cash.[10]

---

[9]   WorldPay. 2022. *The Global Payments Report*. https://worldpay.globalpaymentsreport.com/en.
[10]   Alipay and WeChat Pay are the services in the People's Republic of China. GCash is the service in the Philippines.

Figure 2.3: Global Payment Trend

(a) Global Online (e-commerce) Payment Methods

(b) Global Off-Line (point-of-service) Payment Methods

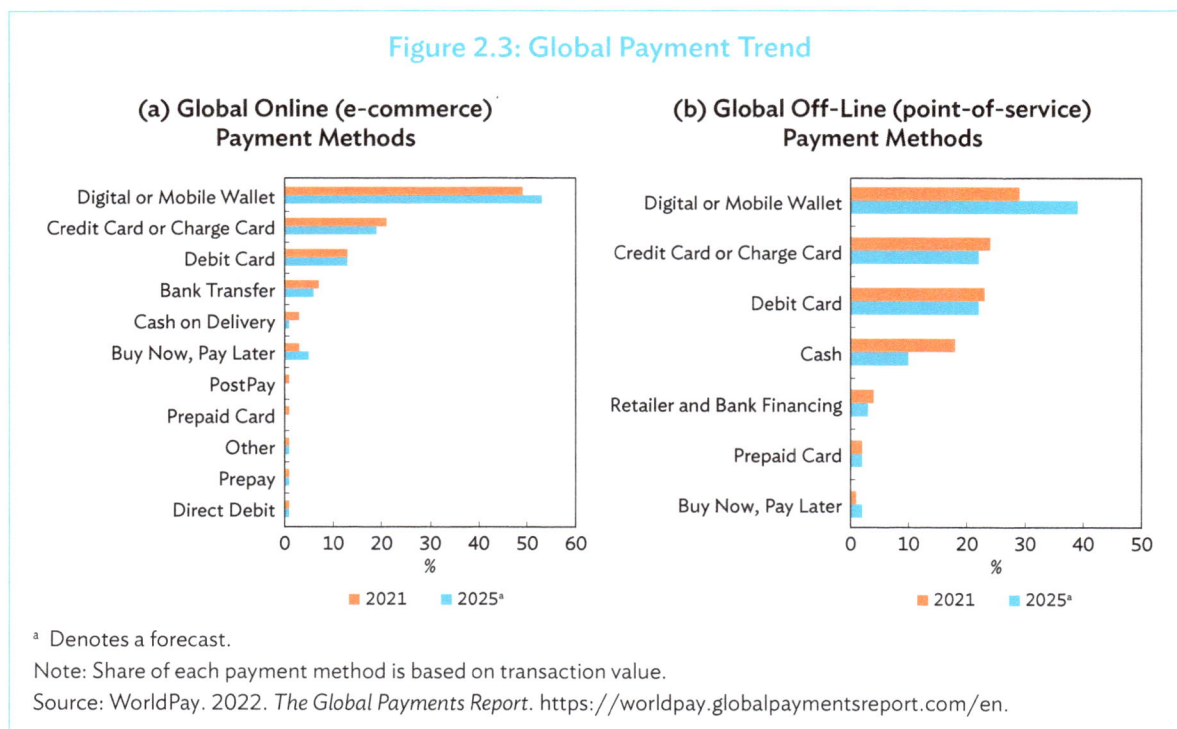

ᵃ Denotes a forecast.

Note: Share of each payment method is based on transaction value.

Source: WorldPay. 2022. *The Global Payments Report*. https://worldpay.globalpaymentsreport.com/en.

FinTech Financing

FinTech financing—which is also referred to as alternative finance and includes peer-to-peer, marketplace lending, balance sheet lending, and crowdfunding—provides financing to individuals and businesses through online channels that have emerged outside the incumbent banking system and traditional capital market. FinTech financing—which can contribute to financial market development, innovation, and inclusion—has been developed based on improvements in digital infrastructure and technology, as well as changing customer expectations for digitally delivered financial services. According to the Cambridge Centre for Alternative Finance (CCAF), global FinTech financing market (excluding the PRC) has grown consistently since 2015: Total transaction volume almost doubled from USD60 billion in 2017 to USD113 billion in 2020 (**Figure 2.4**).[11] The peer-to-peer and marketplace consumer lending model was the largest business model globally in 2020, accounting for a 31% global market share (excluding the PRC), followed by the balance sheet business lending model with a 25% global market share (excluding the PRC). In 2020, the US was the largest market, accounting for 65% of global FinTech financing market volume, followed by the UK with an 11% global market share. Asia and the Pacific (excluding the PRC) comprised an 8% global market share in 2020, while the total value of FinTech financing activities in the region grew by 44% from 2018 to 2020 (**Figure 2.5**). Regarding its contribution to financial inclusion, FinTech activities in sub-Saharan Africa, where 98% of the customer base is either unbanked or underbanked, are showing the potential to improve the financial access of unbanked or underserved groups, even though other regions predominantly cater to banked customers.

---

[11]   T. Ziegler. 2021. *The 2nd Global Alternative Finance Market Benchmarking Report*. Cambridge Centre for Alternative Finance. June. https://www.jbs.cam.ac.uk/faculty-research/centres/alternative-finance/publications/the-2nd-global-alternative-finance-market-benchmarking-report/.

Figure 2.4: Total Global FinTech Volume
(USD billion)

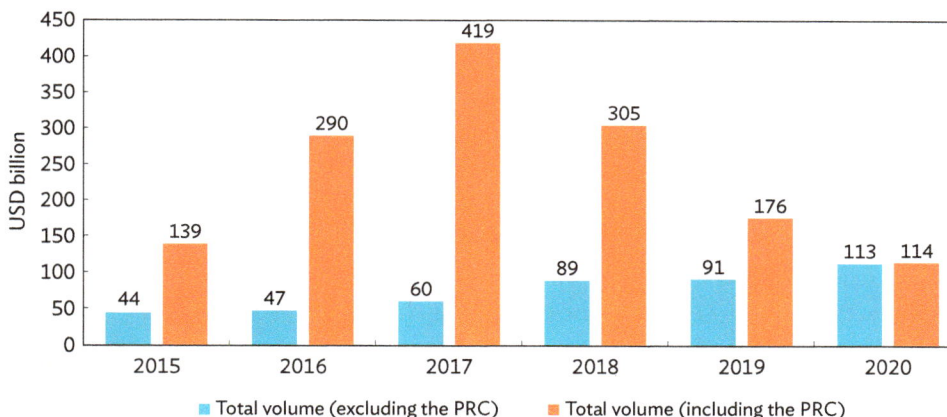

PRC = People's Republic of China, USD = United States dollar.

Note: The online FinTech financing sector in the PRC has shown a drastic decline from USD358.3 billion in 2017 to USD1.2 billion in 2020, with its global market share decreasing by about 84% during this period, mainly due to regulatory tightening and a crackdown on improperly licensed platforms following growing public complaints about high levels of fraud and defaults.

Source: T. Ziegler et al. 2021. *The 2nd Global Alternative Finance Market Benchmarking Report*. Cambridge Centre for Alternative Finance. June. https://www.jbs.cam.ac.uk/faculty-research/centres/alternative-finance/publications/the-2nd-global-alternative-finance-market-benchmarking-report/.

Figure 2.5: FinTech Financing Market Volume in Asia and the Pacific, Excluding the People's Republic of China
(USD billion)

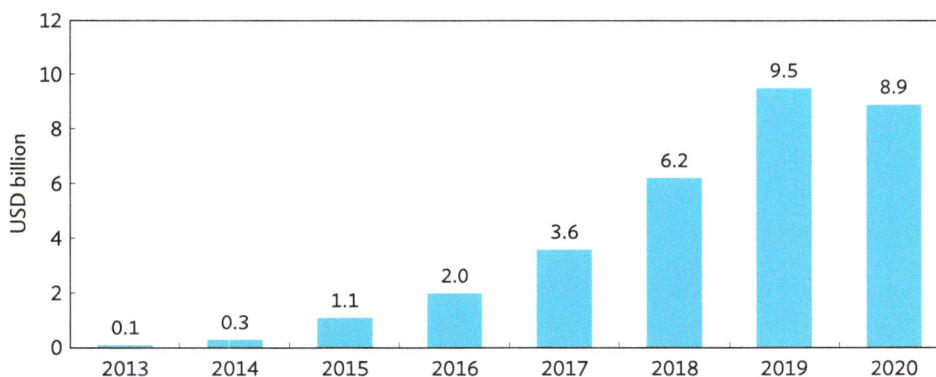

USD = United States dollar.

Source: T. Ziegler et al. 2021. *The 2nd Global Alternative Finance Market Benchmarking Report*. Cambridge Centre for Alternative Finance. June. https://www.jbs.cam.ac.uk/faculty-research/centres/alternative-finance/publications/the-2nd-global-alternative-finance-market-benchmarking-report/.

Robo-Advisor

A robo-advisor is a digital financial advisor that provides financial advice or manages investments with moderate or minimal human intervention. This approach emerged from digital disruption trends in wealth management such as digitally savvy investors, innovative technology, and demand for a superior client experience.[12] Robo-advisors are expected to drive growth based on its benefits, including easy access, lower fees, lower minimum balance requirements, and comprehensive services. According to Statista, assets under management (AUM) by robo-advisors are projected to reach USD1.78 trillion globally in 2022; with an annual growth rate of 15.15%, this is projected to result in a total amount of USD3.14 trillion by 2026, while the number of users is expected to reach 506 million (**Figure 2.6**).[13] The Robo-Advisory Market Report noted that the North American market, which is the largest robo-advisory market, generated a revenue of USD1.61 billion in 2020 and is expected to register a revenue of USD19.48 billion by 2028, while the robo-advisory market in Asia and the Pacific reached USD1.37 billion in 2020 and is expected to register a revenue of USD19.51 billion by 2028 on an average annual growth rate of 41.7% driven by the world's largest and fastest growing middle class in terms of net worth.[14] In the US, Edelman Financial Engines, Vanguard Personal Advisor Services, Schwab Intelligent Portfolio Products, and Betterment comprise a large share of the robo-advisor market, which held a total of USD583 billion in AUM as of March 2021.[15]

Figure 2.6: Global Assets Under Management in the Robo-Advisor Market
(USD trillion)

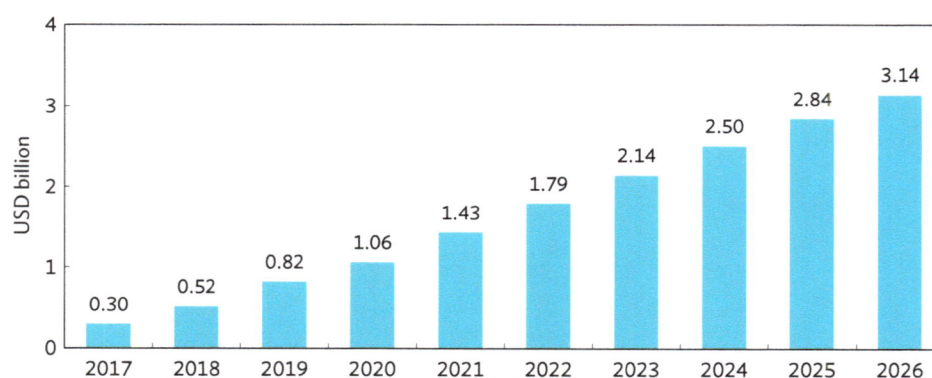

USD = United States dollar.
Source: Statista. Robo-Advisors—Worldwide. https://www.statista.com/outlook/dmo/fintech/digital-investment/robo-advisors/worldwide?currency=usd (accessed 12 September 2022).

---

[12] Deloitte. 2019. *Robots are Here: The Rise of Robo-Advisers in Asia Pacific*. https://www2.deloitte.com/content/dam/Deloitte/sg/Documents/financial-services/sea-fsi-robo-advisers-asia-pacific.pdf.

[13] Statista. Robo-Advisors—Worldwide. https://www.statista.com/outlook/dmo/fintech/digital-investment/robo-advisors/worldwide?currency=usd (accessed 2 December 2022).

[14] ResearchDive. 2022. *Robo Advisory Market Report*. https://www.researchdive.com/8537/robo-advisory-market.

[15] Statista. Value of Assets under Management of Selected Robo-Advisors Worldwide as of March 2022. https://www.statista.com/statistics/573291/aum-of-selected-robo-advisors-globally/ (accessed 12 September 2022).

In Asia and the Pacific, the digital advisory platform Bibit of Indonesia has drawn primarily millennials and first-time investors with digital tools helping users build a portfolio aligned with their goals and risk tolerance. StashAway, of which AUM exceeded USD1 billion as of January 2021, offers digital wealth platforms in Hong Kong, China; Malaysia; and Singapore. Also, Endowus, which received funding from SoftBank, has seen its AUM growth to USD0.74 billion as of June 2021 in Singapore.[16]

Digital Technologies in Financial Services

The advancement of digital technologies is recognized as one of the essential building blocks to enable the digital transformation of traditional banking models by providing benefits such as cost effectiveness, operational efficiency and flexibility, enhanced data analytics, and the facilitation of data sharing. According to the Financial Stability Institute (FSI) and the Financial Stability Board (FSB), these technologies include, but are not limited to, application programming interfaces, artificial intelligence (AI) and machine learning, biometric-based identification and authentication (biometrics), cloud computing and distributed ledger technology (DLT), and mobile devices.[17] The World Economic Forum also suggested that clusters of emerging technologies will unlock unique pathways for innovation in financial services, including the integration of physical and digital processes and reorienting transaction flows.[18] For instance, the cluster consisting of AI, cloud computing, task-specific hardware, the Internet of Things, 5G networking, and DLT enables just-in-time lending for tailored small and medium-sized enterprise lending products and personalized advice proactively and at the moment that unexpected needs arise. To this end, incumbent financial institutions and Fintech firms have been actively investing in digital technologies. In 2022, banks in North America are projected to spend nearly one-half of their total information technology budget on new technology, while European banks are forecast to spend about one-third.[19] Also, digital banking has occupied the largest share among retail banks' information and communications technology spending on service channel improvement across the globe.[20]

Meanwhile, many jurisdictions in Asia and the Pacific have shown continuous digital development in recent years, including a significant increase in mobile phone penetration, which underpins the digital innovation in financial services. However, there is still discrepancy in some areas within the region with regard to information and communications technology access, internet penetration, and the information and communications technology skills of individuals, which will require more collective efforts to attain progress (**Table 2.1**).

---

[16] S. Barquin et al. 2021. Emerging Markets Leap Forward in Digital Banking Innovation and Adoption. *McKinsey & Company*. 23 September. https://www.mckinsey.com/industries/financial-services/our-insights/emerging-markets-leap-forward-in-digital-banking-innovation-and-adoption.

[17] J. Ehrentraud et al. 2020. Policy Responses to FinTech: A Cross-Country Overview. *FSI Insights on Policy Implementation* No. 23. BIS. January. https://www.bis.org/fsi/publ/insights23.pdf; FSB. 2019. *Fintech and Market Structure in Financial Services: Market Developments and Potential Financial Stability Implications*. 14 February. https://www.fsb.org/wp-content/uploads/P140219.pdf.

[18] World Economic Forum. 2020. *Forging New Pathways: The Next Evolution of Innovation in Financial Services*. September. http://www3.weforum.org/docs/WEF_Forging_New_Pathways_2020.pdf.

[19] Deloitte Center for Financial Services. 2019. *2020 Banking and Capital Markets Outlook: Fortifying the Core for the Next Wave of Disruption*. December. https://www2.deloitte.com/content/dam/Deloitte/lu/Documents/financial-services/lu-2020-banking-and-capital-markets-outlook.pdf.

[20] Deloitte Center for Financial Services. 2018. *2019 Banking and Capital Markets Outlook Reimagining Transformation*. September. https://www2.deloitte.com/content/dam/Deloitte/us/Documents/financial-services/us-fsi-dcfs-2019-banking-cap-markets-outlook.pdf.

Table 2.1: Status of Digital Development in Asia and the Pacific

| | ASEAN Member States | | | | | | | | | Non-ASEAN Member States | | | | |
	BN	KH	ID	LA	MY	PH	SG	TH	VN	AU	CN	JP	NZ	KR
Mobile–cellular network coverage (%)	99 (2020)	99 (2020)	98 (2020)	95 (2020)	97 (2020)	99 (2020)	100 (2020)	99 (2020)	100 (2020)	99 (2020)	100 (2020)	100 (2020)	98 (2020)	100 (2020)
Households with Internet access at home (%)	54 (2019)	21 (2017)	78 (2020)	2 (2017)	92 (2020)	18 (2019)	98 (2020)	85 (2020)	76 (2020)	86 (2017)	NA	97 (2020)	77 (2013)	100 (2020)
Mobile–cellular subscriptions per 100 inhabitants	123 (2020)	126 (2020)	130 (2020)	56 (2020)	135 (2020)	137 (2020)	144 (2020)	167 (2020)	143 (2020)	108 (2020)	119 (2020)	154 (2020)	127 (2020)	138 (2020)
Individuals using the Internet (%)	95 (2020)	33 (2017)	54 (2020)	34 (2020)	90 (2020)	50 (2020)	92 (2020)	78 (2020)	70 (2020)	90 (2020)	70 (2020)	90 (2020)	91 (2020)	97 (2020)
Individuals with basic ICT skills (%)	57 (2019)	29 (2017)	49 (2017)	NA	60 (2020)	6 (2019)	53 (2020)	17 (2020)	17 (2019)	NA	NA	59 (2020)	NA	72 (2020)
Individuals with standard ICT skills (%)	40 (2019)	3 (2017)	25 (2017)	NA	42 (2020)	2 (2019)	40 (2020)	10 (2020)	8 (2019)	NA	NA	48 (2020)	NA	51 (2020)

ASEAN = Association of Southeast Asian Nations, AU = Australia, BN = Brunei Darussalam, CN = People's Republic of China, ICT = information and communications technology, ID = Indonesia, JP = Japan, KH = Cambodia, KR = Republic of Korea, LA = Lao People's Democratic Republic, MY = Malaysia, NA = data not available, NZ = New Zealand, PH = Philippines, SG = Singapore, TH = Thailand, and VN = Viet Nam.

Note: Number in parentheses indicates the year of the data.

Source: Digital Development Dashboard of International Telecommunication Union (accessed on 12 September 2022).

As for application of digital technologies in financial services, Asia and the Pacific has actively promoted the digitalization of financial services in line with international trends. While many jurisdictions in the region have sought to utilize emerging technologies such as AI, cloud computing, and blockchain in financial services, some such as Australia, Japan, the Republic of Korea, and Singapore have implemented open application programming interfaces for the sharing and leveraging of customer-permissioned data by banks with third-party developers and firms.[21] According to CCAF, most FinTech firms in the ASEAN region use predictive analytics and machine learning—followed by blockchain and DLT, robotic process automation, and image recognition— while the use of more advanced technologies such as virtual reality, augmented reality, and speech recognition is limited (**Table 2.2**).[22] Given international trends and various initiatives and roadmaps for the region to advance digital finance, the use of digital technologies in financial services will expand more rapidly in the future. This could have a positive impact on digital transformation and the development of financial industries in the region through streamlined cross-border banking and the expansion of customer reach, in addition to the aforementioned merits, provided that relevant matters—including development of digital infrastructure, regulatory harmonization, risk management, information technology risk, cybersecurity, data privacy, outsourcing, and the enhancement of digital literacy— are managed appropriately.

Table 2.2: Technologies Used by Southeast Asian Economies' FinTech Firms (%)

| Technology | Product Category | | | | |
	Artificial Intelligence/ Machine Learning/ Big Data	Capital Raising Crowdfunding	Digital Lending	Digital Payments	Enterprise Technology for Financial Institution
Augmented Reality	4	0	2	2	0
Virtual Reality	4	0	2	0	4
Speech Recognition	13	0	5	2	11
Natural Language Processing	30	6	12	9	19
Deep Learning	39	11	12	5	26
Image Recognition	35	6	20	16	30
Robotic Process Automation	26	22	41	16	26
Blockchain/Distributed Ledger Technology	13	39	7	35	44
Machine Learning	65	22	41	23	48
Predictive Analytics	91	61	76	58	70

Source: Cambridge Centre for Alternative Finance, Asian Development Bank Insitute, FinTechSpace. 2019. *ASEAN FinTech Ecosystem Benchmarking Study*. Cambridge, UK. https://www.jbs.cam.ac.uk/faculty-research/centres/alternative-finance/publications/the-asean-fintech-ecosystem-benchmarking-study/.

---

[21] BIS. 2019. *Report on Open Banking and Application Programming Interfaces (APIs)*. 19 November. https://www.bis.org/bcbs/publ/d486.htm.

[22] Cambridge Centre for Alternative Finance, Asian Development Bank Insitute, FinTechSpace. 2019. *ASEAN FinTech Ecosystem Benchmarking Study*. Cambridge, UK. https://www.jbs.cam.ac.uk/wp-content/uploads/2020/08/2019-ccaf-asean-fintech-ecosystem-benchmarking-study.pdf.

FinTech and Bigtech Companies

New players with digital advantages, FinTech and Big Technology (Bigtech) firms (**Table 2.3**), are increasingly entering the financial industry based on higher customer expectations for digital financial services, technological development, and policies to promote financial innovation and competition. FinTech and Bigtech companies are expected to deliver potential benefits—such as better and more tailored financial services, reduction of transaction costs, enhanced access to financial services (financial inclusion)—and have a positive impact on financial stability due to increased competition. In contrast, they are increasingly attracting the attention of policy makers due to their potential risks, including higher operational risk, increased difficulties in meeting anti-money laundering and combating the financing of terrorism (AML/CFT) requirements, data privacy, outsourcing risk, cyber-risk, liquidity risk, and volatility in bank funding sources.[23] In particular, Bigtech—which comprises large technology companies providing financial services such as Google, Apple, Facebook, and Amazon—could pose more significant challenges to the financial industry and financial stability, including a high degree of concentration or very strong competition in the financial market, systemic risk, and procyclicality of credit provision, which would be based on Bigtech's advantages such as strong

Table 2.3: Financial Services Offered by Bigtech Companies

Bigtech	Main business	Banking[a]	Credit provision	Payments	Crowdfunding	Asset management	Insurance
Google	Internet search/advertising	✓[b]		✓			
Apple	Tech/producing hardware			✓			
Facebook	Social media/advertising			✓			
Amazon	E-commerce/online retail		✓	✓	✓		✓
Alibaba (Ant Group)	E-commerce/online retail	✓	✓	✓	✓	✓	✓
Baidu (Du Xiaoman)	Internet search/advertising	✓	✓	✓	✓	✓	✓
JD.com (JD Digits)	E-commerce/online retail	✓	✓	✓	✓	✓	✓
Tencent	Tech/gaming and messaging	✓	✓	✓	✓	✓	✓
NTT Docomo	Mobile communications	✓	✓	✓	✓		
Rakuten	E-commerce/online retail	✓		✓		✓	✓
Mercado Libre	E-commerce/online retail		✓	✓		✓	

✓ = provision of financial service through Bigtech entity and/or in partnership with financial institutions outside Bigtech group in at least one jurisdiction.
[a] The core activity of an entity engaged in banking is taking deposits, though regulations vary across countries.
[b] Launch was expected in 2021.
Source: J. C. Crisanto, J. Ehrentraud, and M. Fabian. 2021. Big Techs in Finance: Regulatory Approaches and Policy Options. *FSI Briefs* No. 12. March.. https://www.bis.org/fsi/fsibriefs12.pdf.

---

[23]   BIS. 2018. *Sound Practices: Implications of Fintech Developments for Banks and Bank Supervisors. Basel Committee on Banking Supervision*. https://www.bis.org/bcbs/publ/d431.pdf.

network effects, large user base, big data and advanced data analytics, and cross-subsidization.[24] In this regard, a prudent regulatory approach (e.g., activity-based or entity-based regulation) has been discussed internationally, and political momentum is growing to adopt new legislation in the area of competition and antitrust such as the European Union (EU) Digital Markets Act and Digital Services Act.[25]

Meanwhile, a KPMG report shows that total global investment in FinTech companies reached USD210.1 billion across 5,684 deals in 2021 (**Figure 2.7**), which was a 51% increase from USD124.9 billion in 2020.[26] The Americas attracted USD105.3 billion with 2,660 deals, followed by Europe, the Middle East, and Africa (USD77.4 billion, 1,859 deals), and Asia and the Pacific (USD27.5 billion, 1,165 deals) (**Figure 2.8**).

Figure 2.7: Total Global Investment Activity in FinTech Companies (USD billion)

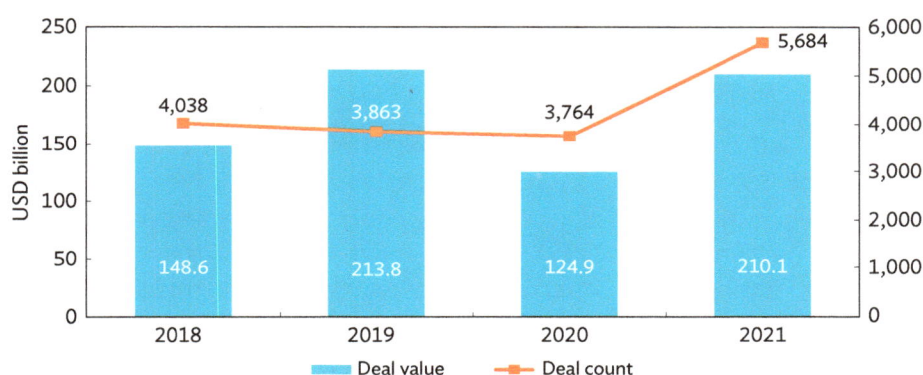

USD = United States dollar.

Note: Data for 2021 as of 31 December.

Source: KPMG International. 2022. *Pulse of Fintech H2'21*. January. https://home.kpmg/xx/en/home/insights/2022/01/pulse-of-fintech-h2-2021-global.html.

---

[24] Organisation for Economic Co-operation and Development (OECD). 2020. *Digital Disruption in Banking and Its Impact on Competition*. https://www.oecd.org/competition/digital-disruption-in-banking-and-its-impact-on-competition-2020.pdf.

[25] J. C. Crisanto, J. Ehrentraud, and M. Fabian. 2021. Big Techs in Finance: Regulatory Approaches and Policy Options. *FSI Briefs* No. 12. March. https://www.bis.org/fsi/fsibriefs12.pdf.

[26] KPMG International. 2022. *Pulse of Fintech H2'21*. January. https://home.kpmg/xx/en/home/insights/2022/01/pulse-of-fintech-h2-2021-global.html.

Figure 2.8: Total Investment Activity in FinTech Companies in Asia and the Pacific
(USD billion)

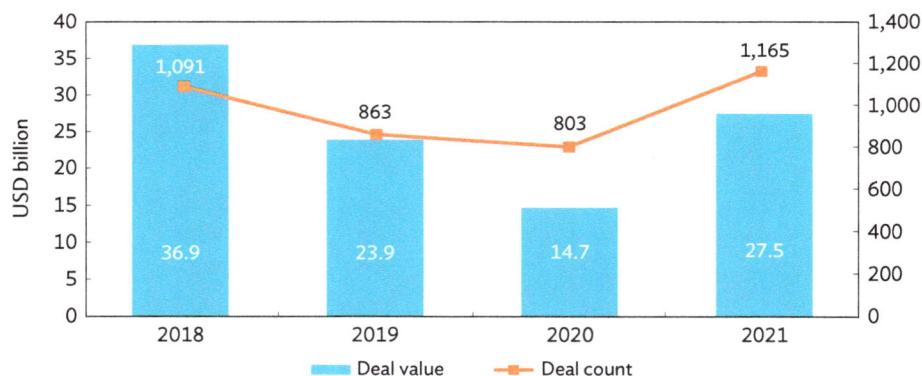

USD = United States dollar.

Note: Data for 2021 as of 31 December.

Source: KPMG International. 2022. *Pulse of Fintech H2'21*. January. https://home.kpmg/xx/en/home/insights/2022/01/pulse-of-fintech-h2-2021-global.html.

According to KPMG and Ernst & Young, the US FinTech market, which ranked first in the Global Fintech Rankings 2021, accounted for 64.9% of total global investment activity in FinTech for 2020 with about 3,000–4,000 FinTech firms (as of 2019), while the UK, which ranked second, comprised 4.8% with about 1,600 FinTech firms (as of 2019).[27] In Asia and the Pacific, Singapore, which ranked fourth in the Global Fintech Rankings 2021, attracted 1.8% of total global investment activity in FinTech for 2020 with about 600 FinTech firms (as of 2019), while Australia, which ranked sixth, accounted for 1.4% with about 600 FinTech firms (as of 2019). Also, CCAF, the Asian Development Bank Institute, and FinTechSpace (2019) noted that in ASEAN member economies, more than USD485 million was invested in 2018 across 68 deals for FinTech start-ups, which represented 143% year-on-year growth from 2017. It is estimated that there are more than 600 FinTech start-ups in the ASEAN region with increasing customer demand for fintech services supported by significant economic potential, high mobile phone penetration levels, and rising internet usage rates (footnote 22).

Cross-Border Digital Financial Services

Cross-Border Digital Payments, Digital Remittances, and Cryptocurrency

Cross-border payments are fund transfers between people or businesses located in different jurisdictions. The money sender typically selects a front-end provider such as a bank or a money transfer operator to initiate the payment. The receiver then gets the payment through the medium designated by the sender. Traditionally, cross-border payments flow through the correspondent banking

27   KPMG International. 2022. *Pulse of Fintech H2'21*. January. https://home.kpmg/xx/en/home/insights/2022/01/pulse-of-fintech-h2-2021-global.html; Ernst & Young. 2021. *UK FinTech: Moving Mountains and Moving Mainstream*. https://assets.ey.com/content/dam/ey-sites/ey-com/en_gl/topics/emeia-financial-services/ey-uk-fintech-2020-report.pdf; InsightsArtist. 2021. 2021 Global Fintech Rankings. December. https://insightsartist.com/2021-global-fintech-rankings/.

network, which most front-end providers use to settle the payment. According to Ernst & Young, the total global cross-border payment volume has grown by about 5% annually since 2018 (**Figure 2.9**). It is expected to reach USD156 trillion in 2022, which consists of business–to–business transactions (USD150 trillion), consumer–to–business transactions (USD2.8 trillion), business–to–consumer transactions (USD1.6 trillion), and consumer–to–consumer transactions (USD0.8 trillion).

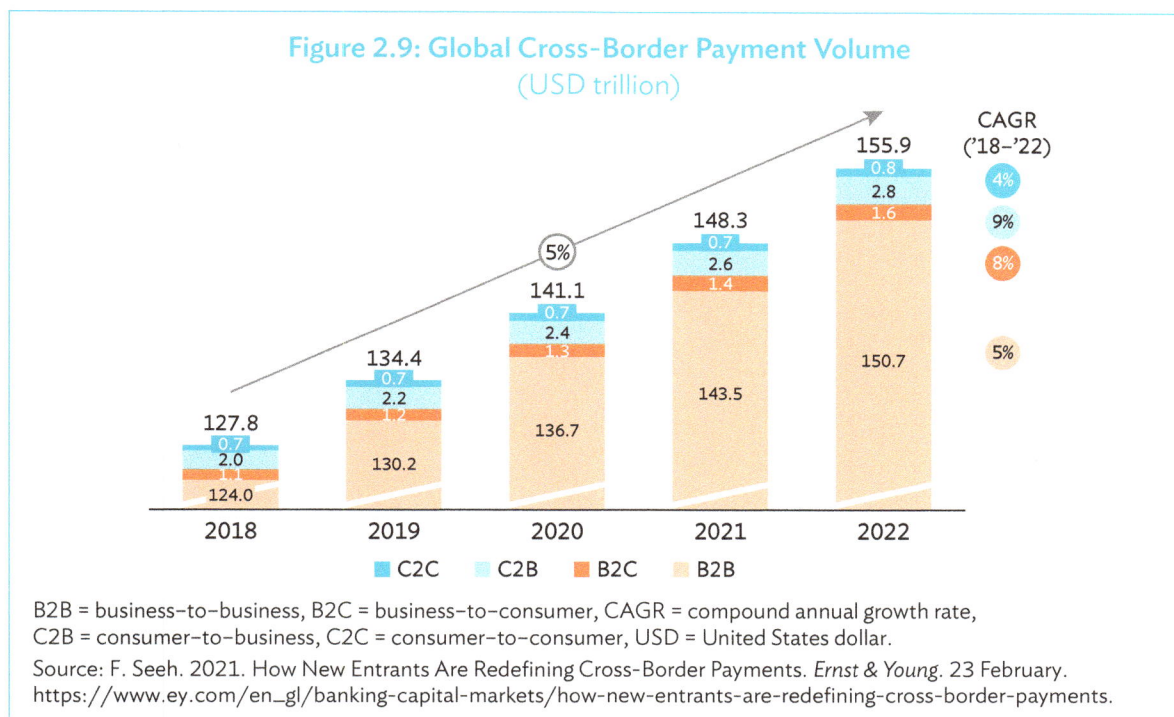

Figure 2.9: Global Cross-Border Payment Volume
(USD trillion)

B2B = business–to–business, B2C = business–to–consumer, CAGR = compound annual growth rate, C2B = consumer–to–business, C2C = consumer–to–consumer, USD = United States dollar.
Source: F. Seeh. 2021. How New Entrants Are Redefining Cross-Border Payments. *Ernst & Young*. 23 February. https://www.ey.com/en_gl/banking-capital-markets/how-new-entrants-are-redefining-cross-border-payments.

In addition, customers are more willing to use digital payment methods to provide faster, cheaper, and more transparent cross-border payment services along with increased penetration of mobile phones and e-money, while global cross-border trade is projected to expand at an annual growth rate of about 5% between 2018 and 2022, most of which will come from emerging markets in Africa, Latin America, and Asia. These trends and traditional issues in cross-border payments—which include high costs, low speed, limited access, and insufficient transparency—have promoted the entry of new specialized players to offer faster, cheaper, and more transparent cross-border digital payment services. Most are focusing on low-value transactions in consumer–to–consumer, business–to–consumer, and business–to–business segments, which are currently underserved by banks and traditional payment providers.[28] In particular, in the cross-border consumer–to–consumer segment (remittances), transaction values are projected to increase by 30% from USD573 billion in 2016 to USD750 billion in 2023 (**Figure 2.10**), of which cross-border digital remittances are expected to comprise more than 50% from 2023.[29] FinTech companies such as Wise, Worldremit, and Remitly have been winning

---

[28] F. Seeh. 2021. How New Entrants Are Redefining Cross-Border Payments. *Ernst & Young*. 23 February. https://www.ey.com/en_gl/banking-capital-markets/how-new-entrants-are-redefining-cross-border-payments.

[29] M. Nicoli and U. Ahmed. 2019. World Bank Blogs. How Digital Remittances Can Help Drive Sustainable Development. https://blogs.worldbank.org/psd/how-digital-remittances-can-help-drive-sustainable-development.

Figure 2.10: Global Cross-Border Remittance Volumes
(USD billion)

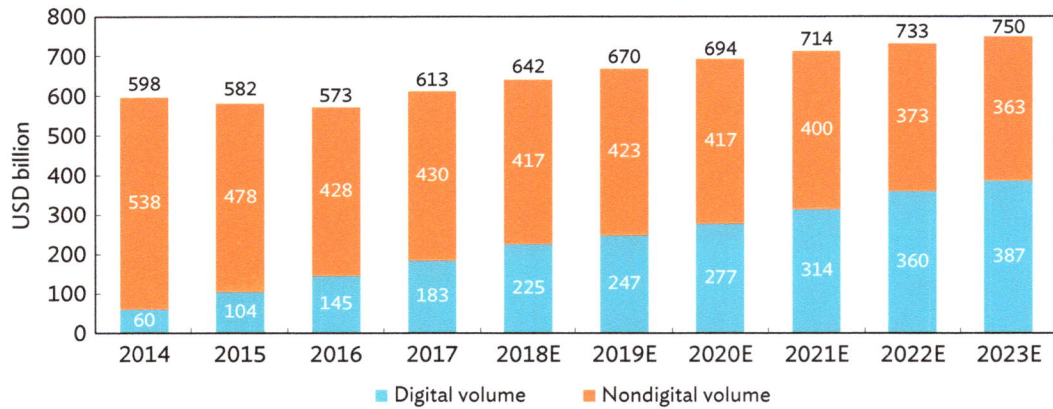

E = estimate, USD = United States dollar.
Sources: Business Insider Intelligence estimates; Juniper Research; M. Nicoli and U. Ahmed. 2019. *World Bank Blogs.* "How Digital Remittances Can Help Drive Sustainable Development." https://blogs.worldbank.org/psd/how-digital-remittances-can-help-drive-sustainable-development.

Figure 2.11: Global Cross-Border Digital Remittances by Fintech Firms
(USD billion)

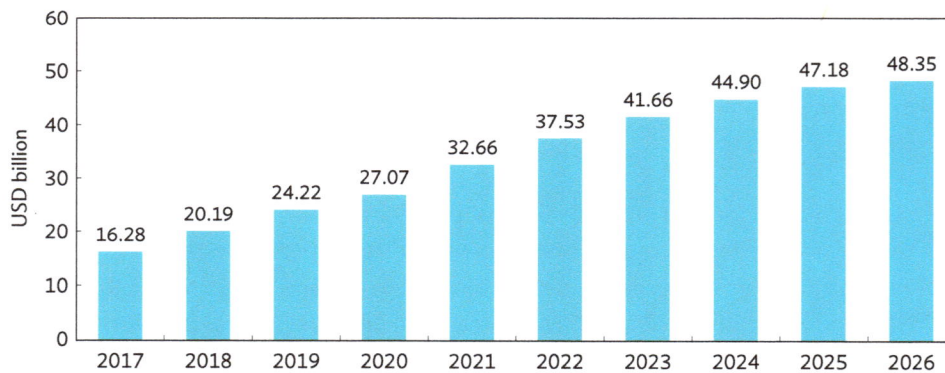

USD = United States dollar.
Source: Statista. Digital Remittances—Worldwide. https://www.statista.com/outlook/dmo/fintech/digital-payments/digital-remittances/worldwide (accessed 12 September 2022).

their market share by offering reduced transfer fees based on optimized use of digital infrastructure (**Figure 2.11**).[30]

In Asia and the Pacific, where remittances are an important source of income for individuals receiving funds from abroad, as well as for many economies as a whole, efforts for faster and more efficient

---

[30] Visa Economic Empowerment Institute. 2021. *The Rise of Digital Remittances: How Innovation Is Improving Global Money Movement.* https://usa.visa.com/content/dam/VCOM/global/ms/documents/veei-the-rise-of-digital-remittances.pdf.

cross-border payments have been growing (**Figure 2.12**). A major cross-border payments initiative in the region is the Asian Payment Network, which was established in 2006 by domestic payment infrastructure providers in ASEAN, with the support of central banks, to establish common standards, guidelines, and collaborative regional efforts for domestic and regional processing and settlement of all digital financial services.[31] Also, ASEAN member states have been pursuing real-time retail payment system cross-border linkages and an ASEAN interoperable quick response code framework.[32] Regarding real-time retail payment system cross-border linkages, the linkage between Singapore's PayNow and Thailand's PromptPay was launched in April 2021.[33] Another link between Malaysia's DuitNow and Thailand's PromptPay was established in June 2021.[34]

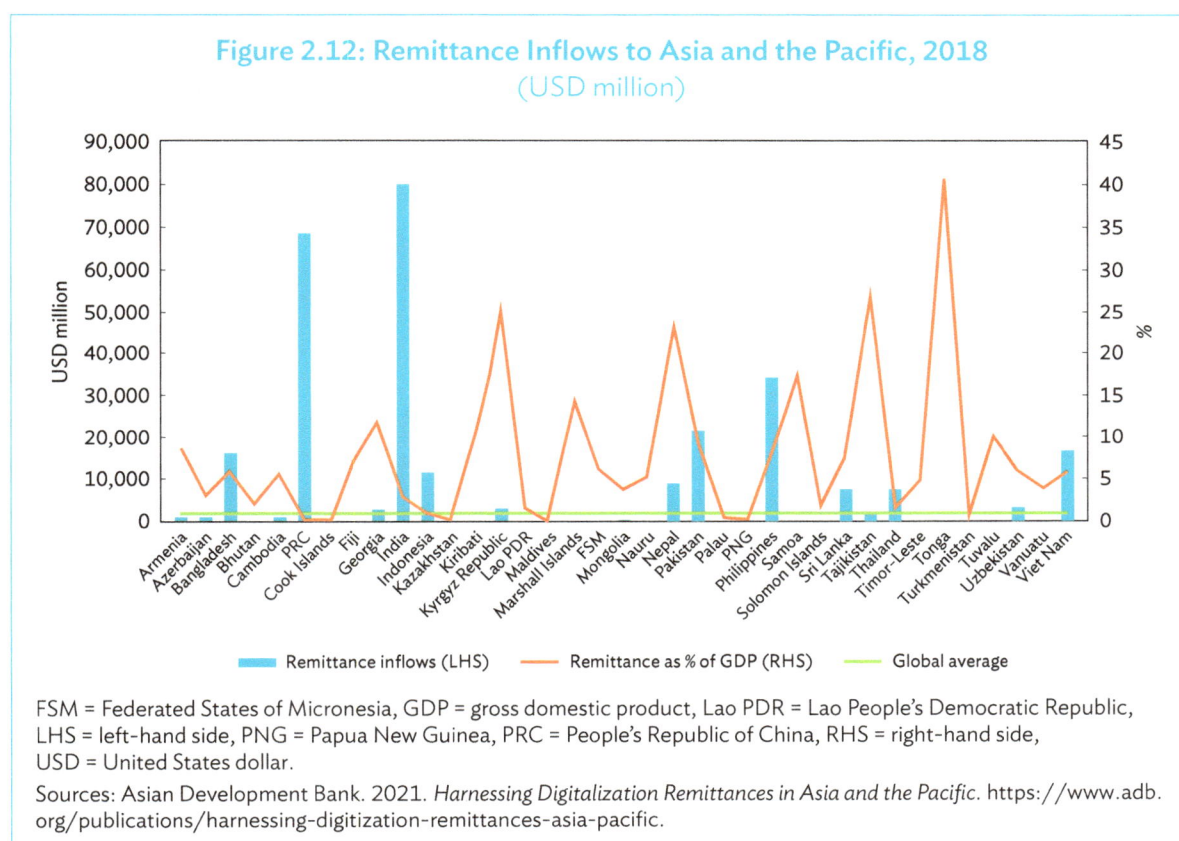

Figure 2.12: Remittance Inflows to Asia and the Pacific, 2018
(USD million)

FSM = Federated States of Micronesia, GDP = gross domestic product, Lao PDR = Lao People's Democratic Republic, LHS = left-hand side, PNG = Papua New Guinea, PRC = People's Republic of China, RHS = right-hand side, USD = United States dollar.

Sources: Asian Development Bank. 2021. *Harnessing Digitalization Remittances in Asia and the Pacific.* https://www.adb.org/publications/harnessing-digitization-remittances-asia-pacific.

---

[31] *Fintechnews Singapore.* 2021. Instant Cross-Border Payments Will Soon Become a Reality in APAC. 30 November. https://fintechnews.sg/57596/payments/instant-cross-border-payments-will-soon-become-a-reality-in-apac/.

[32] ASEAN. 2020. Payment Systems in the Digital Age: Case of ASEAN. *ASEAN Policy Brief* No. 4. April. https://asean.org/wp-content/uploads/2021/09/ASEAN-Policy-Brief-4_FINAL-06Apr2021-1.pdf.

[33] *Monetary Authority of Singapore.* 2021. Singapore and Thailand Launch World's First Linkage of Real-time Payment Systems. 29 April. https://www.mas.gov.sg/news/media-releases/2021/singapore-and-thailand-launch-worlds-first-linkage-of-real-time-payment-systems.

[34] S. Banchongduang. 2021. PromptPay Now Linked to DuitNow. *Bangkok Post.* 19 June. https://www.bangkokpost.com/business/2134811/promptpay-now-linked-to-duitnow.

As the use of cryptocurrencies is increasingly adopted worldwide, the areas of their use have expanded to include digital payments and digital remittances.[35] For example, companies including Microsoft, Starbucks, Tesla, Mastercard, AXA Insurance, Coca Cola, and Expedia have allowed customers to use cryptocurrencies like Bitcoin as an official method of payment for their goods and services.[36] Also, BitPesa, which provides cryptocurrency-based remittances for five currencies across Africa, had transacted USD235 million worth of Bitcoin through April 2021, serving more than 26,000 customers, up from 6,000 in 2017.[37] Coinbase, a US-based cryptocurrency exchange, launched a cryptocurrency remittance pilot program in February 2022 to allow US customers to send cryptocurrencies to recipients in Mexico, who will be immediately able to cash out in their local currency.[38] Furthermore, in 2021, PYMNTS and Stellar Development Foundation conducted a census-balanced survey of 2,079 adult consumers, as representative of the US population, concerning cross-border cryptocurrency remittances (**Figure 2.13**). The survey reported that 23%

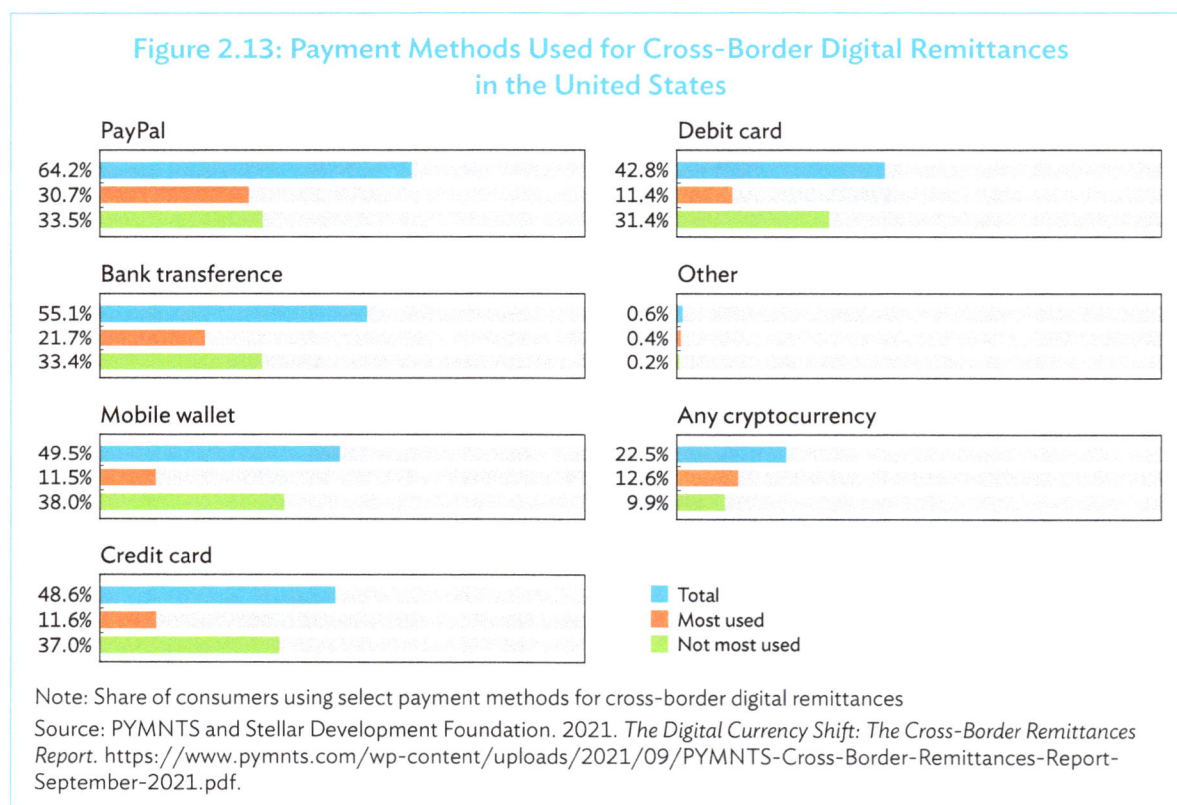

Figure 2.13: Payment Methods Used for Cross-Border Digital Remittances in the United States

PayPal

64.2%	
30.7%	
33.5%	

Debit card

42.8%	
11.4%	
31.4%	

Bank transference

55.1%	
21.7%	
33.4%	

Other

0.6%	
0.4%	
0.2%	

Mobile wallet

49.5%	
11.5%	
38.0%	

Any cryptocurrency

22.5%	
12.6%	
9.9%	

Credit card

48.6%	
11.6%	
37.0%	

- Total
- Most used
- Not most used

Note: Share of consumers using select payment methods for cross-border digital remittances
Source: PYMNTS and Stellar Development Foundation. 2021. *The Digital Currency Shift: The Cross-Border Remittances Report*. https://www.pymnts.com/wp-content/uploads/2021/09/PYMNTS-Cross-Border-Remittances-Report-September-2021.pdf.

---

[35] TripleA, which is a cryptocurrency payment service provider in Singapore, estimated that average global crypto ownership rates are 4.2% with over 320 million cryptocurrency users worldwide as of 2022. It also noted that brands such as Microsoft, Starbucks and PayPal are already accepting cryptocurrency payments. Triple A. Global Crypto Adoption. https://triple-a.io/crypto-ownership-data/ (accessed 6 December 2022).

[36] D. Walsh. 2021. Paying with Bitcoin: These Are the Major Companies That Accept Crypto as Payment. *EuroNews Next*. 4 December. https://www.euronews.com/next/2021/12/04/paying-with-cryptocurrencies-these-are-the-major-companies-that-accept-cryptos-as-payment.

[37] D. Webber. 2021. Cryptocurrency in Cross-Border Payments: After Coinbase's Success, Can Crypto Flourish beyond Assets? *Forbes*. 21 April. https://www.forbes.com/sites/danielwebber/2021/04/21/cryptocurrency-in-cross-border-payments-after-coinbases-success-can-crypto-flourish-beyond-assets/?sh=6bd2e8d6416f.

[38] S. Escobar. 2022. Coinbase Launches Cryptocurrency Remittance Pilot Program in Mexico. *Barron's*. 15 February. https://www.barrons.com/articles/coinbase-cryptocurrency-remittance-pilot-program-mexico-51644952896.

of respondents, representing 8 million adults in the US, had made online payments to friends or family in other countries using at least one kind of cryptocurrency. Many consumers are choosing cryptocurrencies as a payment option to avoid the pain points of cross-border remittances such as high fees and long wait times for processing. In the survey, 13% of customers mentioned that cryptocurrencies were their most used payment method for cross-border digital remittances.

Cross-Border FinTech Financing

With the easy access, convenience, and transparency provided by digital platforms in the FinTech financing sector, it is evident that FinTech financing firms seek to strengthen their global presence and capture further global market share by building international brands and having international websites. According to the 2nd Global Alternative Finance Market Benchmarking Report, released in 2021 by CCAF, the proportion of foreign fundraisers in crowd-led microfinance was 95% (USD160 million), followed by invoice trading with 45% (USD553 million), while a high proportion of foreign fund inflows was reported by donation-based crowdfunding, comprising USD760 million of cross-border transactions (**Figure 2.14**).

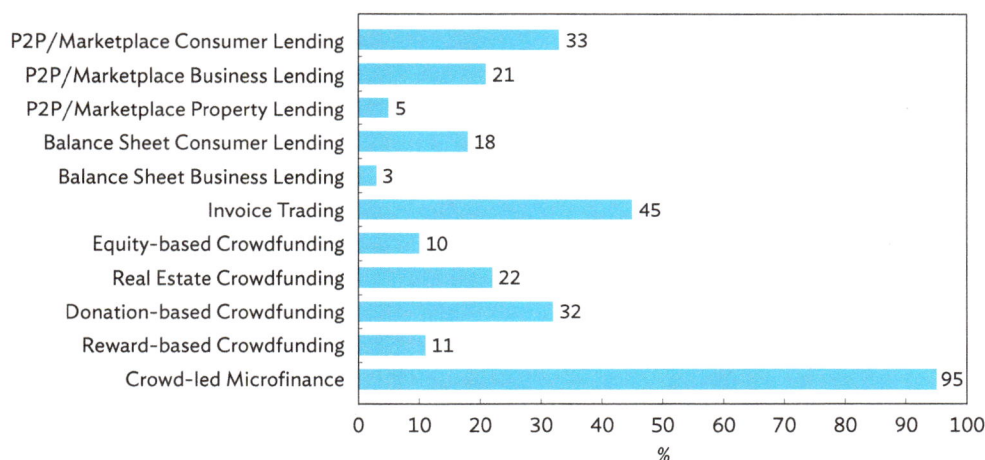

Figure 2.14: Global Cross-Border Transactions of FinTech Financing by Model

P2P = peer–to–peer.
Source: T. Ziegler et al. 2021. *The 2nd Global Alternative Finance Market Benchmarking Report*. Cambridge Centre for Alternative Finance. June. https://www.jbs.cam.ac.uk/faculty-research/centres/alternative-finance/publications/the-2nd-global-alternative-finance-market-benchmarking-report/.

When it comes to cross-border volumes by region (**Figure 2.15**), which include cross-border transactions between countries within the region as well as outside it, sub-Saharan Africa accounted for the highest proportion with 87% (USD162 million) in terms of the ratio of cross-border transactions, followed by Europe with 67% (approximately USD3.3 billion) and Asia and the Pacific with 28% (approximately USD814 million). It is also reported that many FinTech firms in ASEAN consider operating in other ASEAN countries to continue growing. They strongly believe that an enabling

Figure 2.15: Global Cross-Border Transactions of FinTech Financing by Region

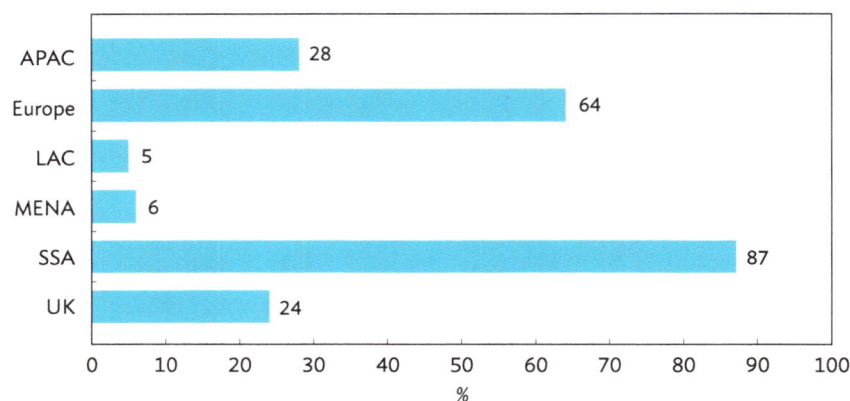

APAC = Asia-Pacific, LAC = Latin America and the Carribean, MENA = Middle East and North Africa, SSA = Sub-Saharan Africa, UK = United Kingdom.
Source: T. Ziegler et al. 2021. *The 2nd Global Alternative Finance Market Benchmarking Report*. Cambridge Centre for Alternative Finance. June. https://www.jbs.cam.ac.uk/faculty-research/centres/alternative-finance/publications/the-2nd-global-alternative-finance-market-benchmarking-report/.

regulatory framework, digital infrastructure readiness, and regulatory innovations (e.g., sandbox) are critical factors to expanding outside their domestic market (footnote 22).

Cross-Border Branchless Banking

In many countries, a foreign bank that falls under local bank licensing requirements must establish a physical presence in the country to engage in banking transactions, including taking deposits or making loans with local residents. However, under the EU's passport regime for banks—which is based on the agreement of all participating states and a common set of rules such as the capital requirements directive, markets in financial instruments directive, and payments services directive applicable in the jurisdictions covered by the passporting arrangement—credit institutions (banks), securities trading firms, and payment and e-money institutions that are authorized in one country of the European Economic Area (EEA) can carry out their cross-border business in another EEA member state through the simplified procedure (**Figure 2.16**) without a physical presence (freedom to provide services).[39] For instance, if a bank, which is authorized in one of the EEA member states, intends to carry out cross-border banking in another EEA member state without the establishment of bank branches under the EU passport system, the bank must notify the host supervisor in the EEA member state where the bank intends to conduct cross-border banking of the intention via its home supervisor, by which the bank is authorized, and go through a relevant assessment.

---

[39] UK Finance. What is Passporting and Why Does it Matter? Brexit Quick Brief No. 3. https://www.ukfinance.org.uk/sites/default/files/uploads/pdf/BQB3-What-is-passporting-and-why-does-it-matter-UKF.pdf.

Figure 2.16: European Passporting Process

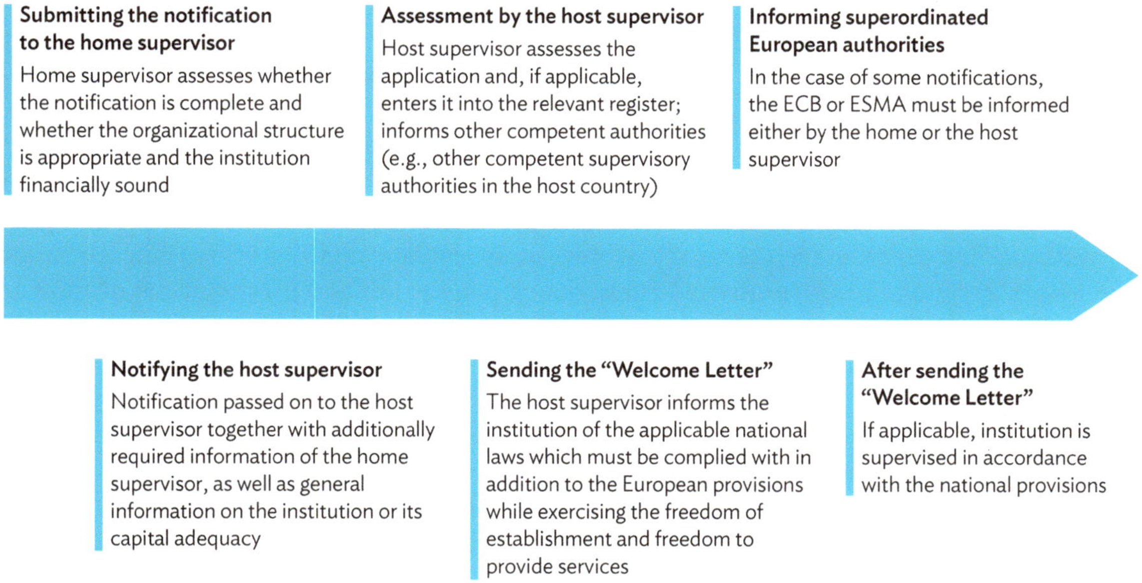

Submitting the notification to the home supervisor
Home supervisor assesses whether the notification is complete and whether the organizational structure is appropriate and the institution financially sound

Assessment by the host supervisor
Host supervisor assesses the application and, if applicable, enters it into the relevant register; informs other competent authorities (e.g., other competent supervisory authorities in the host country)

Informing superordinated European authorities
In the case of some notifications, the ECB or ESMA must be informed either by the home or the host supervisor

Notifying the host supervisor
Notification passed on to the host supervisor together with additionally required information of the home supervisor, as well as general information on the institution or its capital adequacy

Sending the "Welcome Letter"
The host supervisor informs the institution of the applicable national laws which must be complied with in addition to the European provisions while exercising the freedom of establishment and freedom to provide services

After sending the "Welcome Letter"
If applicable, institution is supervised in accordance with the national provisions

ECB = European Central Bank, ESMA = European Securities and Markets Authority.
Source: German Federal Financial Supervisory Authority. Passporting. European Passport. https://www.bafin.de/EN/Aufsicht/BankenFinanzdienstleister/Passporting/passporting_artikel_en.html.

Digital banks, which deliver their banking services primarily over the Internet without relying on branches, have been actively established and operating businesses worldwide to promote innovation, competition, and financial inclusion in the banking industry, which could lead to customer benefits and financial development. For example, Insider Intelligence reported that the share of digital bank account holders in the US will continue to grow from 11.4% (29.8 million) in 2021 to 19.9% (53.7 million) in 2025 based on the growing demand for digital banking services from consumers and increasing trust of digital banks by consumers.[40] Customers of N26, a digital bank headquartered in Germany, exceeded 2 million customers in France in 4 years.[41] Boursorama, the largest digital bank in France in terms of the number of customers, aims to increase its 2.5 million clients to 4.5 million by 2025.[42] The number of customers of Kakao bank and K bank, which are digital banks in the Republic of Korea launched in 2017, reached 14.3 million and 5.4 million, respectively, in April 2021. They also provided 72.8% of the medium-rate loans in the Republic of Korea's banking sector in 2019–2020.[43]

---

[40] *Insider Intelligence.* 2022. What Neobanks Are, How They Work and the Top Neobanks in the US & World in 2022. 9 January. https://www.insiderintelligence.com/insights/neobanks-explained-list.

[41] *N26.* 2021. N26 Exceeds 2 Million Customers in France in 4 Years. 10 June. https://n26.com/en-fr/press/press-release/n26-exceeds-2-million-customers-in-france-in-4-years.

[42] S. Bucak. 2021. French Neobanks Try to Keep It Simple as They Grow Quickly. *Financial Times.* 24 January. https://www.ft.com/content/881bd0a6-96de-4776-818f-f81f2e0230f5.

[43] Financial Services Commission Korea. 2021. Toss Bank (3rd Internet-only Bank) Approved for Banking Business (unofficial translation). 9 June.

According to FSI, a few jurisdictions in Asia and the Pacific—including Malaysia, the Republic of Korea, and Singapore—introduced a specific regulatory framework (**Table 2.4**) for digital banks with some differences between licensing requirements for traditional and digital banks based on policy objectives (e.g., financial inclusion) and digital banks' characteristics, which includes technology-related elements and the aims of the business plan (**Table 2.5**). Most jurisdictions apply existing banking laws and regulations to digital banks. Within Asia and the Pacific, Australia, India, Japan, the PRC, Malaysia, the Philippines, the Republic of Korea, and Singapore have introduced digital banks via existing or specific banking regulatory frameworks. Also, some jurisdictions have implemented transitional schemes to facilitate the establishment of traditional and digital banks (Australia and the UK) or digital banks (Malaysia and Singapore). In such cases, relaxed regulatory requirements for a limited range of business activities are applied to newly authorized banks during entry phase and then a full set of regulatory requirements are applied when starting to trade fully.

Given an enabling environment and the advantage of digital banks, it is expected that this banking model could facilitate and accelerate cross-border branchless banking in the future if relevant arrangements such as passporting and mutual recognition for cross-border digital financial services are properly implemented internationally or regionally. For example, Revolut Bank, which is a digital bank headquartered in Lithuania and part of the UK-based FinTech unicorn Revolut, had been operating banking services in the EEA with a specialized EU banking license obtained through the European Central Bank and the Bank of Lithuania in December 2018. Then the bank was granted a full banking license by the European Central Bank and the Bank of Lithuania in December 2021.[44] According to Revolut and the European Banking Authority Register, the digital bank is providing cross-border branchless banking in 10 European markets—including Belgium, Denmark, Finland, Germany, Iceland, Liechtenstein, Luxembourg, the Netherlands, Spain, and Sweden—under the European passport regime.[45]

Table 2.4: Specific Licensing Frameworks for Digital Banks

Economy	Regulatory status	Transitional Scheme	License Restrictions to Specific Market Segments
Hong Kong, China	Virtual bank	No	None
Korea, Republic of	Internet-only bank	No	Retail and SMEs
Malaysia	Digital bank	Yes	None
Singapore	Digital full bank	Yes	None
	Digital wholesale bank	No	SMEs and other non-retail customers
Taipei,China	Internet-only bank	No	None
United Arab Emirates (ADGM)	Digital bank	No	None

ADGM = Abu Dhabi Global Markets, SMEs = small and medium-sized enterprises.
Source: J. Ehrentraud, D. G. Ocampo, and C. Q. Vega. 2020. Regulating FinTech Financing: Digital Banks and FinTech Platforms. *FSI Insights* No. 27. Bank for International Settlements. 27 August.. https://www.bis.org/fsi/publ/insights27.htm.

---

[44] *PYMNTS*. 2021. Revolut Bank Granted Full EU Banking License amid Criticisms of Unfair Competition. 20 December. https://www.pymnts.com/digital-first-banking/2021/revolut-bank-granted-full-european-union-banking-license-amid-criticisms-unfair-competition.

[45] *Revolut*. 2022. Revolut Launches as a Bank in 10 Western European Markets, Now Available in 28 Countries. 11 January. https://www.revolut.com/news/revolut_launches_as_a_bank_in_10_western_european_markets_now_available_in_28_countries; and European Banking Authority. Credit Institutions Register. https://euclid.eba.europa.eu/register/cir/search.

Table 2.5: Licensing Requirements for Digital Banks

	AE	HK	KR	MY	SG	TC
General licensing requirements						
Legal form and place of incorporation	✓	✓	✓	✓	✓	✓
Ownership structure/control	✓	✓	✓[a]	✓[a]	✓	✓[a]
Long term sustainability of the business plan	✓	✓	✓	✓	✓	✓
Fitness and propriety test	✓	✓	✓	✓	✓	✓
Minimum paid-up capital	✓	✓	✓[b]	✓[c]	✓[c]	✓
Sound risk culture: risk governance frameworks	✓	✓	✓	✓	✓	✓
Exit plan	✓	✓	✓	✓	✓	✓
Technology-related licensing requirements						
Fitness and propriety test on technology fields	–	✓	✓	✓	✓	✓
Track record in technology	–	✓	–	✓	✓	–
Third-party assessment of IT systems	✓	✓	–	✓	–	–
Financial inclusion	✓	✓	✓	✓	✓	–

– = not explicit; ✓ = requirement applies in full from the start; AE = United Arab Emirates; HK = Hong Kong, China; IT = information technology; KR = Republic of Korea; MY = Malaysia; SG = Singapore; TC = Taipei,China.

[a] Requirements on who is allowed to own and/or control digital banks differ from those applicable to traditional banks. In Malaysia, while not a mandatory requirement, preference is given to applicants where the controlling equity interest resides with Malaysians.
[b] Internet-only banks have a minimum capital requirement of KRW25 billion; other banks KRW100 billion.
[c] Compliance not required in full in the initial phase of transitioning schemes.

Source: J. Ehrentraud, D. G. Ocampo, and C. Q. Vega. 2020. Regulating FinTech Financing: Digital Banks and FinTech Platforms. *FSI Insights* No. 27. Bank for International Settlements. 27 August. https://www.bis.org/fsi/publ/insights27.htm.

Box 2: Digital Wallet

A digital wallet (or mobile wallet) is a financial transaction application that runs on mobile devices and securely stores customers' payment information. It allows customers to make online, in-app, and in-store payments, as well as fund transfers so that they do not need to carry a physical payment medium such as a credit card, debit card, or cash.

How It Works

Digital wallets, which are largely classified into card-based digital wallets and stored-value digital wallets, use a mobile device's wireless capabilities like Bluetooth, Wi-Fi, and magnetic signals to transmit payment data securely from a mobile device to a point-of-sale (POS) designed to read the data and connect via these signals. The technologies used by mobile devices and digital wallets are as follows:

(i) **Quick Response codes.** Quick Response (QR) codes are matrix bar codes that store information. A camera of mobile device and a scanning system of a digital wallet are used to initiate payment.

(ii) **Near field communication.** This technology allows two mobile devices to connect and transfer information using electromagnetic signals. It requires two mobile devices to be within about 1.5 inches (4.0 centimeters) from each other to connect.

(iii) **Magnetic secure transmission.** This is the same technology used by magnetic card readers that read your card when you swipe it through a slot on a POS. A customer's mobile device generates an encrypted field that the POS can read.

The payment information, which customers store in digital wallets and choose to use for a transaction, is transmitted from the customers' device to the POS terminal, which is connected to payment processors. Then, through the processors, gateways, acquirers, or any other third parties involved in payment transactions, the payment is routed through card networks, banks, or payment service providers to make a payment. Digital wallets are also being used online using QR codes and integrated checkout processes that enable consumers to complete purchases on their mobile device.

Trend in Asia and the Pacific

As of 2020, the population of Asia and the Pacific had surpassed 3.5 billion, which accounted for around 48% of the world's total population. Digital wallets usage is projected to increase from 1.8 billion users (42.1% of the region's total population) in 2020 to 2.6 billion users (58.6%) in 2025. The transaction volume is expected to increase from 377 billion transactions in 2020 to 636 billion in 2025, while total transaction value is forecasted to increase from USD4.1 trillion in 2020 to USD7.0 trillion in 2025. Also, the competition in respective markets is intensifying, with notable leaders such as AliPay and WeChat Pay in the People's Republic of China; OVO, ShopeePay, LinkAja, and GoPay in Indonesia; PayPay in Japan; Kakao Pay in the Republic of Korea; GrabPay in Malaysia and Singapore; GCash and PayMaya in the Philippines; TrueMoney in Thailand; and MoMo in Viet Nam.

Sources: N. Kaissi. 2021. Mobile Wallets Will Reach 2.6 Billion Users in Asia Pacific by 2025. *The Asian Banker*. 28 October. https://www.theasianbanker.com/updates-and-articles/mobile-wallet-will-reach-2.6-billion-users-in-asia-pacific-by-2025; J. Kagan. 2021. Digital Wallet Explained: Types with Examples and How It Works. *Investopedia*. 10 April. https://www.investopedia.com/terms/d/digital-wallet.asp; Statista.

BANKING REGULATION AND SUPERVISION IN THE DIGITAL ERA | 3

This section examines how banks should be regulated and supervised in the financial digital era. Since the global financial crisis (GFC) in the late 2000s, a variety of financial regulatory and supervisory reforms have been discussed and implemented to effectively respond to the increasingly complicated nature of cross-border banking activities, together with the emergence of the non-bank financial sector in the global financial system. We briefly review these reforms as they contain valuable implications for digital banking and then introduce the recent regulatory and supervisory efforts by global financial authorities to enjoy the benefits of banking digitalization and address the associated risks.

Overview of Development in Financial Regulation and Supervision since the Global Financial Crisis

During the GFC, the collapse of the US subprime mortgage market triggered global financial system instability. Failing to stem the contagion of this negative impact on the global economy, financial authorities around the world faced significant financial regulatory and supervisory challenges. For example, in terms of financial regulation, there were insufficient regulations on banks and financial intermediation. There were no data to monitor over-the-counter derivative transactions; there was little monitoring of financial intermediation by the non-bank financial sector such as shadow banking; and there was insufficient global supervision of large banking groups operating across jurisdictions.

Prior to the GFC, global financial regulatory efforts were primarily made by the Basel Committee on Banking Supervision (BCBS), the International Organization of Securities Commissions, and the International Association of Insurance Supervisors. They were largely independent and worked with financial authorities of each member's jurisdiction on banking, securities, and insurance, respectively. In 2009, immediately after the GFC, the Financial Stability Forum was strengthened under an agreement among members of the Group of Twenty (G20) and then reorganized as the FSB. With the support of the G20, the FSB has served as an "international control tower" on financial regulation, overseeing international organizations operating independently, promoting global financial regulatory reforms, proposing action plans, and reporting the results to the G20.

The FSB-led financial regulatory reforms have taken two broad approaches—reinforcing existing entity-based regulations and introducing new activity- or risk-based regulations—to strengthen regulations across the entire financial system. Entity-based regulations include strengthened Basel capital requirements and new liquidity requirements for internationally active banks under the

Basel III agreement, increased total loss-absorbing capacity of global systematically important financial institutions (G-SIFIs), and the introduction of recovery and resolution plans. These were responses to the "too big to fail" problem accompanying large-scale injections of public funds that emerged as an emergency response during the GFC and were criticized afterward. On the other hand, the regulations on banking entities at the time did not sufficiently address securitization and re-securitization, derivatives, securities lending, repurchase agreements, and other transactions that triggered the crisis, as well as excessive risk-taking behavior in the non-bank financial sector, which was under lax regulation. For this reason, the FSB focused on the activity of financial intermediation and aimed to introduce activity- or risk-based regulations. For example, in securitization, retention regulations were introduced in which originators or arrangers held part of the credit risk of the underlying assets to prevent moral hazard associated with the credit risk transfer. Regarding securities lending and repos, the minimum haircut requirements were introduced to prevent the haircut rate from rapidly increasing in the event of market stress, leading to significant deteriorations in market functioning.

The FSB has also enhanced the monitoring of non-bank financial intermediation, which is often called shadow banking, based on one of the lessons from the GFC.[46] The FSB began to collect, share, and disclose information on non-bank financial intermediation from member jurisdictions, thereby increasing the transparency of financial intermediation by the non-bank financial sector that had previously been difficult to grasp. In addition to developing recovery and resolution plans for G-SIFIs, the FSB introduced a framework for information sharing among related authorities by the Crisis Management Group, which is chaired by home financial authorities. Moreover, major financial authorities have launched supervisory colleges based on the new financial monitoring principles proposed by the BCBS.[47] The supervisory colleges are a new framework for sharing supervisory information and issues with the financial authorities of each jurisdiction and hosted by the home financial authorities of the major banking groups that are active internationally. Thus, a mutual monitoring system for the major banking groups was established and strengthened. In this manner, since the GFC, the supervision and monitoring of G-SIFIs has been significantly strengthened under the leadership of the FSB and the BCBS, with the cooperation of financial authorities in each jurisdiction.[48]

Since the GFC, the introduction of activity- or risk-based regulations, and the supervision and strengthening of cooperation among financial authorities, have become new trends. These trends have useful implications for the regulatory and supervisory framework in the financial digitalization era, which will be discussed in the following subsections.

---

[46] BIS FSB. 2011. *Shadow Banking: Strengthening Oversight and Regulation*. Basel. https://www.fsb.org/wp-content/uploads/r_111027a.pdf.

[47] BIS BCBS. 2010. *Good Practice Principles on Supervisory Colleges*. Basel Committee on Banking Supervision. https://www.bis.org/publ/bcbs170.pdf.

[48] During this period, as shown in BIS CGFS. 2017. Designing Frameworks for Central Bank Liquidity Assistance: Addressing New Challenges. *CGFS Papers No. 58*. Basel, active discussions also took place among central banks around the world on how they should provide liquidity assistance and cooperate in the case of a financial crisis.

Emerging Regulatory and Supervisory Issues in the Digital Financial Landscape: Basic Principles

Referring to the report by the Bank for International Settlement (BIS) in February 2018, *Sound Practices: Implications of Fintech Developments for Banks and Bank Supervisors*, we provide guidance on how financial regulation and supervision should respond to the rapid progress of financial digitalization, with a particular focus on the banking sector.[49]

The enhancement and implementation of financial regulation and supervision after the GFC, which was reviewed in the previous subsection, can be interpreted from a broad perspective as a result of the progress in financial globalization and cross-bordering, the increasing interconnectedness of the financial system among jurisdictions, and the increasing complexity of risks inherent in financial instruments. Meanwhile, as discussed in Section II, progress in financial digitization has provided existing banks with opportunities to pursue profits by improving their information management and processing capabilities and by commercializing costs through the effective use of digital technology (FinTech). In addition, non-bank firms with advantages in digital technology and information infrastructure have been increasingly entering the business traditionally handled by banks (TechFin). What should the basic principles of the digital age then be for financial authorities, who are in a position to regulate and supervise the changing competitive environment surrounding banking businesses?

First, the progress of financial digitalization is a great opportunity for the financial industry as a whole. While being aware of the risks involved, technological innovation in the financial services market should not be fundamentally impeded, and a free and competitive environment should be sufficiently ensured. As introduced in the above-mentioned BIS 2018 report, financial authorities in each jurisdiction are pursuing a variety of measures to promote financial innovation (**Table 3**). Through such implementation experiments, financial authorities are expected to fully examine the advantages and disadvantages (risks) of technological innovation from a neutral standpoint and to make efforts not only to realize financial inclusion and improve the efficiency of payments and settlements, but also to support sustainable economic growth from a financial perspective.

Second, it is necessary to ensure the effectiveness of banking supervision while paying attention to the balance between promoting financial innovation and maintaining financial system stability. In this context, we believe that the introduction of new regulations should be cautious, except when it is vital to keep a level playing field between new and old entities and to prevent crime. In terms of a level playing field, banking operations in the digital age are increasingly dependent on outsourcing, including to firms outside the banking group.[50] Under these circumstances, the existing regulations and

---

[49] This project was launched by the BCBS in 2016 as a working group, and the report was released in 2018 following public consultation in 2017. During this period, other international organizations also examined the policy implications of the development of financial digitalization. For example, the FSB analyzed the impact of financial digitalization on the financial system stability from a macroprudential perspective in the June 2017 report, *Financial Stability Implications from FinTech: Supervisory and Regulatory Issues that Merit Authorities' Attention*, taking into account the changes in settlement and market infrastructure. The International Monetary Fund in 2017 published the Staff Discussion Note, *Fintech and Financial Services: Initial Considerations*, to present the challenges for the financial sector and regulatory and supervisory authorities in the digital age from the perspective of financial system stability.

[50] A good example would be credit scoring that was traditionally conducted by banks internally but has increasingly been made by non-bank firms within their financial groups and even by those outside the groups, taking advantages of modelling and AI technologies.

Table 3: Initiatives to Promote Innovation by Jurisdiction

| | Innovation Hub
A place to meet and exchange ideas | Innovation Facilitator | |
		Accelerator Boot-camp for start-ups, culminating in a pitch presentation	Regulatory Sandbox Testing in a controlled environment, with tailored policy options
Australia	ASIC	ASIC	ASIC
Belgium	NBB/FSMA		
ECB	SSM		
France	ACPR/AMF	BDF	
Germany	BaFin		
Italy	BOI		
Hong Kong, China	HKMA	HKMA	HKMA/SFC/IA
Japan	BoJ/FSA		
Korea, Republic of	FSC		FSC
Luxembourg	CSSF		
Netherlands	DNB/AFM		DNB/AFM
Poland	FSA		
Singapore	MAS	MAS	MAS
Switzerland	Finma		Finma
United Kingdom	BoE/FCA	BOE	FCA

ACPR = Autorité de contrôle prudentiel et de resolution, AFM = Netherlands Authority for the Financial Markets, AMF = Autorité des marchés financiers, ASIC = The Australian Securities and Investments Commission, BaFin = The Federal Financial Supervisory Authority, BDF = Banque de France, BoE = Bank of England, BOI = Bank of Italy, BOJ = Bank of Japan, CSSF = Commission de Surveillance du Secteur Financier, DNB = De Nederlandsche Bank, FCA = Financial Conduct Authority, Finma = Swiss Financial Market Supervisory Authority, FSA = Financial Services Agency, FSA (Poland) = Financial Supervision Authority, FSC = Financial Services Commission, FSMA = Financial Services and Markets Authority, HKMA = Hong Kong Monetary Authority, IA = Insurance Authority, MAS = Monetary Authority of Singapore, NBB = National Bank of Belguim, SFC = Securities and Futures Commission of Hong Kong, SSM = Single Supervisory Mechanism.
Source: Bank for International Settlements, Basel Committee on Banking Supervision. 2018. *Sound Practices: Implications of Fintech Developments for Banks and Bank Supervisors.* 19 February. https://www.bis.org/bcbs/publ/d431.htm.

supervision of bank entities may not be sufficient to deal with the risks faced by the financial system as a whole. Therefore, financial authorities should have some form of supervisory accessibility not only to existing banks but also to FinTech and new TechFin firms.[51]

Third, coordination and cooperation among relevant authorities will become increasingly important to ensure the effectiveness of banking supervision in the financial digitalization era. Specifically, it is necessary to strengthen cooperation with authorities other than banking supervision, which is in charge of information security, intelligence, competition policy, and consumer protection in each

---

[51] In this regard, financial authorities, such as the European Banking Authority and the Financial Services Agency of Japan, recently requested banks to strengthen their monitoring of outsourced operations because such information technology firms are beyond the responsibilities of financial supervision and regulations, while the Bank of England, in contrast, rather tends to supervise such non-bank firms directly.

jurisdiction. In addition, as digital services further accelerate the cross-border provision of financial services and increase associated cross-border risks, it is necessary to continue to address the issue of enhancing international cooperation among financial authorities. To fully respond to the unknown risks and uncertainties brought about by financial digitalization, the relevant authorities should share their knowledge and experience with the aim of enhancing supervisory tools and methods.

Fourth, and perhaps most important, is the development and ensuring enough of human resources in charge of bank supervision in the era of financial digitalization. The authorities should develop staff with a certain level of FinTech literacy and flexibly transform banking supervision practices to be more effective and efficient.[52] In this respect, we are entering an age in which it is desirable to reform rigid internal personnel and promotion systems and to introduce digital training and flexible personnel exchange and recruitment systems that transcend industry boundaries.

Desirable Changes in Regulation and Supervision along with the Transformation of the Traditional Banking Model

Taking into account the major direction of banking regulation and supervision in the era of financial digitalization, we examine several important regulatory and supervisory issues and how to respond to them in the new age.

Ensuring a Level Playing Field

In most jurisdictions, new digital banks are subject to the same regulations as existing banks, regardless of differences in the delivery methods and channels of financial services.[53] The idea behind this is that even if digital technology unbundles existing banking services, the risks they pose and their impact on financial system stability are basically the same. However, some jurisdictions have adopted a flexible approach, such as allowing a grace period after entry until full compliance with regulatory and supervisory standards is achieved (Australia) and gradually expanding tradable operations according to compliance capabilities (UK). In addition, according to the European Central Bank, some supervisors in Europe are seeking to improve risk management by adding specific guidance and licensing requirements for new firms whose business model is centered on financial technology.[54] In any case, under the basic principle that financial innovation and free competition should not be hindered and that financial system stability should be maintained, each jurisdiction should ensure a level playing field between existing banks and new entrants.

---

[52] Not all but some of the staff in charge of banking supervision need to understand the most recent FinTech and TechFin trends and updated information on cybersecurity and, as discussed later, acquire the necessary skills for RegTech and SupTech developments.

[53] For example, J. Ehrentraud, D. G. Ocampo, and C. Q. Vega. 2020. Regulating FinTech Financing: Digital Banks and FinTech Platforms. *FSI Insights* No. 27. Bank for International Settlements. 27 August. https://www.bis.org/fsi/publ/insights27.htm.

[54] European Central Bank. 2018. *Guide to Assignments of Fintech Credit Institution License Applications*. https://www.bankingsupervision.europa.eu/ecb/pub/pdf/ssm.201803_guide_assessment_fintech_credit_inst_licensing. en.pdf.

Bank Licensing

Most jurisdictions do not, in principle, give special treatment to the licensing standard, which is the most fundamental element of banking regulation. However, as according to the survey conducted by the BIS, there are some jurisdictions that impose restrictions on transition measures and the scope of operations, depending on the services provided.[55] Since these new entrants are highly dependent on information technology (IT), some jurisdictions require additional criteria such as transaction and customer data, outsourcing management, and contributions to financial inclusion.

From Entity-Based to Activity- or Risk-Based Regulation and Supervision

Financial digitization has led to the unbundling of banking businesses by significantly reducing the cost of individual banking activities. In the past, deposit and loan operations were the core source of revenue, and banks additionally provided other services that were less profitable. However, in the age of digitization, the effects of economies of scale and scope have made it possible to operate many of them as a single profit opportunity.

As long as existing banks utilize digital technology to enhance their services, there is no problem with continuing the existing entity-based style of regulation and supervision. Even in the case of strengthening cooperation and business alliances within the banking group, and even in the case of outsourcing certain banking operations outside the group, the necessity of the significant reforms of the regulatory and supervisory framework is considered to be small by requiring banks to enhance the risk management of third parties. The BIS also pointed out the rationale of entity-based regulation and supervision in this context by arguing: "[T]he main rationale of the current regulatory approach is that the safety and soundness of each institution depend on all the activities it performs and the way they interact with each other. To the extent that the combination of those activities creates risks beyond the sum of those associated with each of the activities, a group-wide, entity-based approach is warranted."[56]

In recent years, however, the need for activity- or risk-based regulation and supervision has been discussed. Behind this is the emergence of entities that specialize in, for example, providing credit scoring, loan assessment, fund settlement, remittance, and even business matching, all of which have traditionally been part of banking services. Many of them are TechFin firms that do not belong to the existing banking sector but that are, if they were to be categorized, information and technology firms that enter into financial services. Even in these operations, risks related to financial system stability, AML/CFT, cyberattacks, personal information leakage, and investor protection remain unchanged basically, and thus the regulation of capital and liquidity to some extent and the enhancement of operational risk management should be encouraged. Whether virtual or not, regulators need to check risks involved in a new business carefully. The risk profile of new banking business may be different from conventional business, but the risk mitigation measures, such as requiring appropriate regulatory capital levels against the risk evaluated, continue to be effective.

---

[55] J. Ehrentraud, D. G. Ocampo, and C. Q. Vega. 2020. Regulating FinTech Financing: Digital Banks and FinTech Platforms. *FSI Insights* No. 27. Bank for International Settlements. 27 August. https://www.bis.org/fsi/publ/insights27.htm.

[56] F. Restoy. 2021. FinTech Regulation: How to Achieve a Level Playing Field. FSI Occasional Papers No. 17. Bank for International Settlements. 2 February. p. 8. https://www.bis.org/fsi/fsipapers17.htm.

Our conclusion is that, in consideration of the scope of business operations and the magnitude of potential risks, while based on an entity-based approach, new entrants should be treated flexibly and appropriately with activity- or risk-based regulation and supervision, depending on the authority's financial strategies and plans. This is because applying the entity-based style without any consideration would impose an excessive cost burden and impede financial innovation.[57] Digitalization is unbundling banking services; thus, a regulatory approach also needs to transform. Digital banking service providers may focus on payment and thus may not take credit risk. In such a case, the traditional approach to charging an additional capital buffer for the risk may not be sufficient. As they become key market infrastructures, any stoppage of their system would cause significant economic damage to society; hence, regulators may need to ask them to invest in multiple layers of safeguard measures instead of additional capital charges to manage the impact of increasing operational risk. In cases where a platformer with a huge amount of customer information, often called BigTech, takes over an existing bank or establishes a major financial group, it may be desirable to apply the existing entity-based regulations and supervision in light of the significant influence on the entire financial system. Calvo et al. (2018) reviewed changes in the institutional designs of financial sector oversight after the GFC. They found various changes in the arrangement of financial sector authorities (i.e., banking, insurance, and securities business). They concluded that there is no ideal organization for financial supervision, but it is better to organize fit-for-purpose arrangements based on periodic assessments to facilitate information flows and adequate coordination across relevant parties in light of prevailing supervisory objectives.[58]

Cyber Security and Cyber Resilience as Bigger Threats to Digital Finance

The expansion of e-payments during the COVID-19 pandemic accelerated digital transformation, but it also heightened the risk of cyberattacks and cybercrime. The volume of cybercrime has been on an upward trend and will continue to rise. Cyber criminals are more organized than ever before, and they share resources and expertise. Per the International Criminal Police Organization (INTERPOL): "Cybercrime has become a multibillion-dollar industry, and the profits are appealing to traditional crime syndicates interested in diversifying their criminal activities by including use of the virtual ecosystem for communication and money exchange, but also for committing cybercrime."[59] Besides, the impact of system disruptions caused by cyberattacks as well as human error and natural hazards would be proliferated beyond borders as e-payments are interconnected.

---

[57] One possible benchmark is how potentially large new entrants could influence financial system stability. However, even if their business is limited, if supervisors recognize their potential risks (e.g., cross-border connectivity, operational influences on market infrastructure, and currency mismatch), entity-based supervision would still be effective regardless of their balance sheet size and business scope, although the numerical criteria is difficult to set in advance.

[58] D. Calvo et al. 2018. Financial Supervisory Architecture: What Has Changed after the Crisis? *FSI Insights* No. 8. Bank for International Settlements. 30 April. https://www.bis.org/fsi/publ/insights8.htm.

[59] INTERPOL. 2021. *ASEAN Cyberthreat Assessment 2021: Key Cyberthreat Trends Outlook from the ASEAN Cybercrime Operations Desk*. Singapore. https://www.interpol.int/en/News-and-Events/News/2021/INTERPOL-report-charts-top-cyberthreats-in-Southeast-Asia.

Need for Further Coordination and Collaboration among Financial Regulators

FinTech is unbundling traditional banking services and creating new services. Traditional regulatory divisions of labor among financial sectoral regulators may create an unnecessary regulatory overlap, while there may be a risk of overlooking possible important regulatory issues. Therefore, inter-agency information exchanges within a country as well as at the regional level need to be considered.

Cooperation and collaboration among relevant authorities will become increasingly important to mitigate the risks associated with the advancement of financial digitalization. Cybersecurity necessitates urgent coordination among all financial regulatory authorities within a country as well as the region. Based on the comparison of various cybersecurity regulations across jurisdictions, FSB (2017) noted that conflicting, or even similar but not identical, requirements in the regulations would create an adverse effect. For example, there may be slight differences in regulations in timetables for required notification to regulators with respect to security incidents, penetration testing requirements, governance, data leakage protection, and two-factor authentication requirements that result in higher regulatory compliance costs in different jurisdictions. In addition, potential conflicts between privacy law requirements and cybersecurity requirements not only increase administration costs but also may force the separation of a network in a particular jurisdiction to insulate it from the parent and other subsidiaries.[60]

To respond to a variety of risks that are expected to increase with digitization, it may also be necessary to expand the scope of coordination with nonfinancial authorities. Examples include the issues of AML/CFT and know-your-customer and know your customer's customer (KYC/KYCC), responding to cyberattacks, protecting personal information, and protecting retail investors from AI and robotic advisors. Meanwhile, it should not be forgotten that wide-area power outages caused by natural hazards are a significant threat in the digital age, as well as an insufficient and unstable IT communications environment.

In the US, the Financial Services Sector Coordinating Council was established in 2002 by financial institutions to work collaboratively with key government agencies such as the Department of the Treasury, Department of Homeland Security, Federal Deposit Insurance Corporation, Federal Reserve Board of Governors, Office of Comptroller of the Currency, Securities and Exchange Commission, Federal Bureau of Investigation, and US Secret Service. Through these relationships, the council directly assists the sector's response to natural hazards, threats from terrorists, and cybersecurity issues of all types.[61]

Effective solutions and strengthening resilience to organized cyberattacks and unexpected cyber disruption may require collaboration not only among financial regulators but also with the banking industry and private sector security experts. Cybercriminals can move beyond borders while authorities are confined to work within their jurisdictions, which may create a lag in reaction to their attacks. The jurisdiction is primarily determined by the location of the offenders, victims, and impacts of

[60] FSB. 2017. *Summary Report on Financial Sector Cybersecurity Regulations, Guidance and Supervisory Practices*. Basel. 13 October.
[61] Financial Services Sector Coordinating Council. https://fsscc.org/about-fsscc/.

cybercrime. To address this, domestic cybercrime laws should be applied even though the offenders' activities, locations of victims, and affected jurisdictions may extend beyond borders. Unfortunately, the situation cannot be changed quickly; thus, smooth and effective collaboration and coordination among government agencies as well as the private sector will be more important than ever.

SupTech, RegTech, and Promotion of Data Standardization

In response to the progress of financial digitalization, financial authorities need to promote financial innovation in the market by improving the efficiency and sophistication of regulations and supervision called RegTech and SupTech, respectively.

Financial digitalization is inevitable as corporate activities and economic transactions go global and digital. In recent years, the compliance burden for AML/CFT and KYC/KYCC has been increasing, and the expected penalties and reputational risks have become enormous.

Under these circumstances, it is no exaggeration to say that reducing compliance costs for reporting to financial authorities and regulations is an important issue that affects the jurisdiction's financial competitiveness. It is imperative for financial authorities to reduce the burden of paper-based reporting and respond to online reporting. To some extent, a KYC process can be digitalized by a combination of various authentication technologies so that physical presence may not be required. The shift to online reporting will eliminate the burden of overlapping reporting by financial institutions, depending on the jurisdiction, and will also facilitate information sharing between authorities. More recently, there have been attempts to use AI to detect anomalous transactions and initiatives, such as allowing the authorities to join distributed ledger nodes to collect the information and data they need automatically.

To facilitate communications among the financial authorities, it is necessary to establish a framework of data exchange across different authorities within a country as well as within a region. The authorities need to establish common regulatory perspectives and understanding. The discussion can start with the standardization of regulatory information and data. This will facilitate the comparison of data within the same sector (i.e., banking, insurance, and capital markets) as well as comparison across the sectors. Common data definitions, templates, and data models will help with data gathering and sharing. It will also enhance consistency and understanding across authorities.

In fact, significant differences in data reporting requirements—including data format, data elements, definitions, and reporting thresholds—have been identified as impediments to information sharing across jurisdictions. Besides, the differences will increase the compliance cost associated with financial institutions' cross-border operations. The differences also have the potential to impair data quality, usability, and ease of aggregation in ways that hinder authorities' ability to analyze global data sets. Firms' reporting burdens could be eased via the adoption of common reporting definitions or templates.[62]

---

[62] FSB. 2019. *FSB Report on Market Fragmentation*. Basel. https://www.fsb.org/2019/06/fsb-report-on-market-fragmentation-2/#:~:text=The%20report%20lays%20out%20approaches,work%20to%20address%20market%20fragmentation.

Given the different state of digitalization, some jurisdictions may not be ready to accept new banking services from the other jurisdictions. But it is desirable to discuss some level of technical specification and guidelines regionally because these can facilitate access to different markets and support a quick catch-up. In addition, standardization may expand economies of scale; thus, it would lead to cost reductions for service recipients in less developed markets. For example, ASEAN may be able to consider more active participation in the International Organization for Standardization (ISO) standard discussions. In Asia, the People's Bank of China, the Bank of Japan, and the Bank of Korea represent to the ISO Technical Committee 68 (TC68). TC68 is responsible for creating global standards for core banking, capital markets, asset management, payments, credit card processing, and information security specific to financial services. Active participation in TC68 would facilitate establishing a common understanding of various new technologies and devices as well as IT risk management. This would create the basis for more an open technological environment across the region.

Regarding data protection, a growing number of countries have introduced or are considering introducing restrictions to the movement of data outside of their national borders. These restrictions range from strict localization requirements that force companies to locally store and process the data generated inside a country to specific conditions that need to be met to move data abroad. For example, Indonesia, Malaysia, and Viet Nam have data localization requirements that vary in scope. In the EU, the new General Data Protection Regulation requires that recipient countries outside of the EU offer an adequate "level of protection" or that certain legal clauses are introduced into the private contracts that underlie the data transfers. If uncoordinated restrictions of data portability continue, this will increase the costs of cross-border operations and impede regional financial and banking integration.

These restrictions limit the internal sharing of data for risk management, cybersecurity, and AML/CFT, as well as the development of global technological and outsourcing solutions. This is particularly relevant for cloud computing technologies, which provide both cost and technological benefits for organizations that adopt such solutions to enhance product and service offerings to customers since the interconnected data centers are generally distributed in different jurisdictions. Cloud computing not only leads to greater efficiency gains in the form of economies of scale, but it also helps to mitigate traditional IT risks such as capacity and resiliency.[63]

Although divergences in data-related regulations across jurisdictions are justifiable in relation to different policy goals and security concerns, regional coordination would help avoid the unnecessary and costly fragmentation of database management. In particular, uncoordinated data fragmentation would increase the risk of overlapping and overlooking important regulatory issues.

---

[63] Institute of International Finance. 2019. *Addressing Market Fragmentation: the Need for Enhanced Global Regulatory Cooperation*. Washington, DC. January. https://www.iif.com/portals/0/Files/IIF%20FSB%20Fragmentation%20Report.pdf.

In addition, efforts to address the issues of AML/CFT and KYC/KYCC with the adoption of legal entity identifiers (LEIs) would be more effective with the shift to an online regulatory and supervisory environment.[64] The 2021 Financial Action Task Force survey highlighted the need for increased cooperation between regimes to standardize sanction list formats, the interpretation of contents, expected responses associated with listings, and approaches to list distribution. The survey showed the preference for the greater use of structured identifiers such as LEIs to simplify the screening process and improve detection performance.[65]

---

[64] The LEI is a 20-character alphanumeric code defined by ISO in accordance with ISO 17442. Key information that can be referenced by the LEI allows for the clear and unique identification of the entities participating in financial transactions. Since each LEI contains information about the ownership structure of the entity, it provides answers to the questions of "who is who" and "who is whose parent company," and contributes to greater transparency in the global market. It will prevent market misconduct and financial fraud, and thus promote market soundness and address the issues of AML/CFT and KYC/KYCC. The FSB emphasizes that the adoption of a global LEI will help achieve multiple financial stability objectives, including improved internal risk management and appropriate risk assessment.

[65] Financial Action Task Force. 2021. *Cross-Border Payments Survey Results on Implementation of the FATF Standards*. https://www.fatf-gafi.org/publications/fatfrecommendations/documents/cross-border-payments.html.

4 RISKS AND MITIGATION MEASURES FOR MORE DIGITALLY INTEGRATED REGIONAL FINANCIAL MARKETS

In the age of digitization, financial transactions will become more globalized, crossing borders easily. A variety of new firms are expected to enter different markets. In addition, financial innovation will reduce the need for physical branches, and the traditional concept of headquarters and operational bases will fade. In the context of ASEAN+3, in which the economies are increasingly integrated, it is necessary to consider potential implications for cross-border banking and the possible provision of cross-border digital financial services. Banking regulations inevitably involve country-specific aspects unless we have a banking union. There are good reasons that financial regulators are divided by different sectors of financial services because the focus of regulatory interests may not always be the same, though all regulators aim to maintain financial stability. However, cyberspace makes conflicts of geographical as well as functional jurisdictions more complex. If a digital financial service expands widely in the region, the overall impact of system failure on the region's economies could be very large. If a system stoppage in one market causes a failure of payment in other markets, it may cause another failure; then, it could lead to a cumulation of unsettled amounts, and then a financial crisis. This section examines the impact of conflict of jurisdictions in cyberspace, revisits the basic principles for the home and host supervisory arrangements, and proposes regional risk mitigation measures focusing on liquidity to supplement the function of the lender of last resort. Though financial services may go beyond borders, financial regulations must be applied based on jurisdictions. It is important to consider regional risk mitigation measures along with the expansion of new financial services before any crisis happens.

Financial Integration and Conflict of Jurisdictions in Cyberspace

Digital transformation is expected to enhance financial services in a much cheaper, easier, and geographically wider manner. However, further utilization of technologies—such as the Internet, big data, cloud sourcing, and distributed ledger—may pose difficult questions to regulators. Various digital finance services can be provided without a physical premise; thus, it raises questions of who should regulate and how. These questions may complicate the process of financial integration because there would be a possible conflict of jurisdictions or a vacuum of jurisdiction because it is difficult to set clear international borders in cyberspace.

The term jurisdiction can be considered to cover the following three categories: (i) jurisdiction to prescribe (i.e., a country's ability to make its law applicable to persons, conduct, relations, or interests); (ii) jurisdiction to adjudicate (i.e., a country's ability to subject persons or things to the process of its courts or administrative tribunals); and (iii) jurisdiction to enforce (i.e., a country's ability to induce or compel compliance or to punish noncompliance with its laws or regulations).[66] Jurisdiction can be exercised based on one of the following: (i) territoriality (i.e., conduct taking place within the country's territory or designed to have effects within the country's territory); (ii) nationality (i.e., conduct performed by the country's nationals); (iii) passive personality (i.e., conduct having the country's nationals as its victims); (iv) protective principle (i.e., conduct directed against a country's vital interests); and (v) universality (i.e., conduct recognized by the community of nations as of "universal concern" such as genocide, torture, piracy, aircraft hijacking, hostage-taking, war crimes, and the slave trade) (footnote 66). Based on these, a financial services regulator can consider whether it can or needs to enact regulation on a targeted financial service, whether it can enforce the regulation, and whether it can or should exercise its regulatory power over the financial institutions providing the service.

Traditionally, banking regulation is based on territoriality. Banks are licensed and supervised by regulators in the jurisdiction where a bank is established and located. The 1975 BCBS *Report on the Supervision of Banks' Foreign Establishments*, also known as the Basel Concordat, states that "each country has a duty to ensure that foreign banking establishments in its territory are supervised."[67] The BCBS *Minimum Standards for the Supervision of International Banking Groups and Their Cross-Border Establishments* states that "all international banking groups and international banks should be supervised by a home country authority that capably performs consolidated supervision" and "the creation of a cross-border banking establishment should receive the prior consent of both the host country supervisory authority and the bank's and if different, banking group's home country supervisory authority."[68] Home country means where the controlling parent is located. The host country is where the foreign affiliate of a banking group is located. Effective supervision on cross-border banking is primarily based on cooperation between home and host country supervisors. BCBS (1996) tried to mitigate the problem of conflict of jurisdictions by improving information flows between home and host country supervisors.[69] To enhance the supervision of global systemically important banks, multilateral working groups of relevant home and host country supervisors were established as supervisory colleges to enhance information exchange and cooperation. Supervisory colleges are expected to enhance the mutual trust and appreciation of needs and responsibilities on which supervisory relationships are built.[70]

In many jurisdictions, a foreign bank that falls under local bank licensing requirements must actually establish a physical presence in the country and use such an establishment to engage in banking transactions such as taking deposits or making loans with local residents. However, under the European passport procedure of the EU, based on mutual recognition, cross-border retail e-banking services can be offered in Europe through a largely simplified licensing procedure without a physical presence.[71]

---

[66] American Society of International Law. 2014. "Jurisdictional, Preliminary, and Procedural Concerns," in *Benchbook on International Law* § II.A, edited by Diane Marie Amann. www.asil.org/benchbook/jurisdiction.pdf.

[67] BCBS. 1975. *Report on the Supervision of Banks' Foreign Establishments*. https://www.bis.org/publ/bcbs00a.pdf.

[68] BCBS. 1992. *Minimum Standards for the Supervision of International Banking Groups and Their Cross-Border Establishments*. https://www.bis.org/publ/bcbsc314.htm.

[69] BCBS. 1996. *The Supervision of Cross-Border Banking*. Basel. https://www.bis.org/publ/bcbs27.htm.

[70] BCBS. 2010. *Good Practice Principles on Supervisory Colleges*. Basel. https://www.bis.org/publ/bcbs177.htm.

[71] BCBS. 2003. *Management and Supervision of Cross-Border Electronic Banking Activities*. BIS. Basel. https://www.bis.org/publ/bcbs99.htm.

In 2003, the BCBS published a paper on management and supervision of cross-border electronic banking activities (foonote 70). Given various advancements in computing and information and communication technologies, we now see more new and different financial services, but the basic principles of supervision considered for e-banking should be applicable even under the current circumstances. BCBS (2003) recognized that "international banks provide e-banking products and services to their customers in different countries through the websites of their licensed bank branches or banking subsidiaries in those countries. Such e-banking activity is strictly an extension of their existing international banking business to include the Internet delivery channel in their respective local markets. Accordingly, these e-banking transactions are local transactions subject to the law and jurisdiction of that country."[72] However, the BCBS continued: "[T]he open, ubiquitous, and automated nature of the internet implies that neither geography nor time poses significant barriers between banks and their e-banking customers. Consequently, while most banks offer their e-banking products and services exclusively to their home market and to foreign markets where they have local licensed banking establishments, a number of banks also have begun to conduct cross-border e-banking activities; that is, the provision of online banking products or services remotely from one country to residents in another country" where the banks do not have a licensed banking establishment yet (footnote 72). Therefore, BCBS (2003) recognized "the essential role of effective supervision of cross-border banking activities by the home country supervisor in cooperation with local supervisors of countries within whose borders the subject bank operates."[73]

It is desirable to recognize the responsibility of home country supervisors on the extraterritorial provision of financial services outside of the home country, even if there is no physical banking presence in a local jurisdiction. Home country supervisors need to ensure the financial institutions providing financial services virtually should not violate local regulations and properly inform the local authorities.[74]

Second, local supervisors need to consider whether the financial services provided are damaging or pose any risk to the local interest or not. Given the open nature of the Internet, information regarding digital financial services and products on the financial institutions' websites is accessible from anywhere globally; thus, the simple availability of information neither constitutes a cross-border offering of financial service nor violates the legitimate supervisory interest of a local authority. In other words, regulators need to consider what kind of service would constitute their material supervisory interest—such as economic and financial stability and consumer and investor protection—and on what condition their jurisdiction can be exercised and enforced.

If a financial institution conducts financial services virtually and does not have a competent and effective home country supervisor, the local supervisor where the financial services are provided to residents may wish to explore granting a local license and imposing additional requirements to conduct from a

---

[72]   Footnote 70, p. 2.

[73]   Footnote 70, p. 3.

[74]   BCBS. 1992. *Minimum Standards for the Supervision of International Banking Groups and Their Cross-Border Establishments* states "the home country supervisory authority should receive consolidated financial and prudential information on the bank's or banking group's global operations, have the reliability of this information confirmed to its own satisfaction through on-site examination or other means, and assess the information as it may bear on the safety and soundness of the bank or banking group."

local subsidiary.[75] This would allow the host supervisor to ring-fence the foreign entity's activities in its jurisdiction and supervise them. Given the virtual nature of the digital financial service delivery channel, a refusal to grant a local license might not be effective. To increase the effectiveness of the supervision, the local supervisors may consider possible coordination and collaboration with other supervisors, of which residents are also exposed to the services. Multilateral supervisory enforcement would put pressure on financial institutions to ensure compliance with applicable local laws, regulations, and requirements (**Box 4.1**).

It is difficult to set a clear national border in cyberspace, but banking regulations continue to be applied and governed based on territoriality. To mitigate a possible gap and unexpected risks, an appropriate home and host supervisory arrangement remains an effective and practical approach to manage the expansion of cross-border digital financial services. There will be more cases where closer coordination between home and host supervisors is required.

Box 4.1: E-Banking Service without a Local License or Establishment and Consideration for Local Banking Supervisors

When contacted by a foreign bank that intends to provide e-banking services to local residents but does not have a local license or establishment, the local supervisor needs to consider the following:

   (i)   whether the cross-border e-banking activities are subject to effective home country supervision;

   (ii)   whether there is an existing adequate process for supervisory dialogue between the respective supervisors on the foreign bank's activity;

   (iii)   the need to discuss with the foreign bank its intentions and plans—possibly including a discussion with the foreign bank's home supervisor(s) about any identified risks or concerns—and to explore an appropriate framework for coordination and cooperation, if necessary;

   (iv)   the need to inform the foreign bank of the applicability of any relevant local banking laws, regulations, or requirements; and

   (v)   the need to inform the foreign bank's home supervisor (if any) of how it intends to ensure the bank's compliance with relevant local banking laws, regulations, or requirements.

If a situation arises wherein a local bank supervisor determines that a foreign bank with no local presence is conducting cross-border e-banking activities in violation of local laws, regulations, or requirements, it needs to consider the following options:

   (i)   informing the foreign bank of any noncompliance with local laws or regulations;

   (ii)   informing the foreign bank's home country banking supervisor (if any) of the situation;

   (iii)   publicly advising local residents that the foreign bank is conducting cross-border ebanking business in violation of local laws and regulations; or

   (iv)   taking any appropriate enforcement actions.

Source: Basel Committee on Banking Supervision. 2003. *Management and Supervision of Cross-Border Electronic Banking Activities*. Basel.

---

[75] Practically, it would be difficult to impose a penalty or sanction on the subject institution. Most likely, the regulator can consider banning the service.

Principles for the Home and Host Supervisory Arrangement

As mentioned, cyberspace makes the conflict of jurisdictions more complicated. It is important to manage regulatory issues arising from cross-border banking and financial services through an appropriate home and host supervisory arrangement. Building trust and confidence in peer regulators is the basis of any effective cross-border regulatory cooperation. Supervisory colleges are organized to establish such trust and an effective process of information exchange. They play a valuable role in the supervision of internationally as well as regionally active banks by assisting members in developing a more comprehensive understanding of a bank's risk profile and providing a framework for addressing topics that are highly relevant to the supervision of the group (**Box 4.2**). [76]

Currently, supervisory colleges are organized to support the effective supervision of particular international or regional banking groups. Given the expansion of cross-border digital financial services, it may become necessary to expand the scope of the colleges and form various levels of groups to ensure effective communication among the authorities in the region. When new services are provided, it is necessary to establish a common understanding of risk profiles and risk mitigating measures to the new services. As banking services are unbundled and recomposed in various ways, a home supervisor may need to share supervisory tools and monitoring with a host supervisor to ensure effective monitoring of cross-border banking. To promote the cross-border offering of new banking services, a home supervisor may need to provide assurance to a host supervisor by sharing information through regional supervisory colleges and crisis management groups. Through effective communication and information exchange between home and host supervisors, a capacity gap between them can be mitigated; thus, a regulatory gap and unnecessary regulatory overlap can be avoided. If regulations significantly differ between jurisdictions where financial institutions are based (home) and where digital financial services are provided (host), regulatory arbitrage may occur more easily than before. For this reason, global and regional harmonization of financial regulations will become more important than ever, and it is thus desirable to further strengthen cooperation and coordination among financial authorities.[77]

Importance of Cross-Border Liquidity Management

The expansion of cross-border banking and digital payment services may reduce the central banks' ability to act as the lender of last resort (LOLR), a provider of liquidity to a financial system or a bank that is solvent but temporality illiquid; hence, it would pose an additional systemic risk to the region. Extending banking and financial service networks beyond borders may bring wider and more efficient services. But it is not clear whether and to what extent the central banks can support troubled foreign branches and subsidiary networks jointly. Even if the home central bank wants to support a troubled financial institution, its support could not be extended beyond the border as its ability to provide foreign currencies is limited. In addition, a single failure in one market can be transmitted to other markets.

---

[76] BCBS. 2015. *Progress Report on the Implementation of Principles for Effective Supervisory Colleges*. Basel.

[77] The basic agenda of supervisory colleges reflects the necessary contents to be shared and harmonized between home and host supervisors, including domestic and global business strategies of the financial groups; their risk assessment (e.g., results of stress testing and cyberresilience); and the functionality of the executive board and audit committee. Meanwhile, to what extent domestic policy concerns should be preserved is an important and sensitive issue, such as in the area of intelligence, and thus should be discussed on a case-by-case manner.

Box 4.2 Principles for an Effective Supervisory College

Principle 1: College Objectives

Supervisory colleges should enhance, on an ongoing and confidential basis, information exchanges and cooperation among supervisors to support the effective supervision of international banking groups. Colleges should enhance the mutual trust and appreciation of needs and responsibilities on which supervisory relationships are built.

Principle 2: College Structures

Supervisory colleges should be structured in a way that enhances effective oversight of international banking groups, taking into account the scale, structure, and complexity of the banking group, its significance in host jurisdictions, and the corresponding needs of its supervisors. While a college is a single forum, multiple or variable substructures may be used given that no single college structure is likely to be suitable for all banks.

Principle 3: Information Sharing

College members should do their best to promptly share appropriate information with respect to a banking group's principal risks, vulnerabilities, and risk management practices. Mutual trust and willingness to cooperate are key for effective two-way information sharing. To facilitate this process, supervisory colleges should strive toward confidentiality agreements among college members such as those contained in memoranda of understanding.

Principle 4: Communication Channels

Communication channels within a college should ensure the efficiency, ease of use, integrity, and confidentiality of information exchange. The home supervisor should make sound communication channels available to the college and host supervisors should use them appropriately and regularly.

Principle 5: Collaborative Work

Supervisory colleges should promote collaborative work among members, as appropriate, to improve the effectiveness of the oversight of international banking groups. Collaborative work should be by agreement among supervisors and should recognize national legal constraints.

Principle 6: Interaction with the Institution

Interaction between the college members and the banking group should complement the interaction that individual supervisors (both home and host) have with the specific entity they supervise.

Principle 7: Crisis Preparedness

Supervisory colleges are distinct from but complementary to crisis management and resolution structures. The work of a banking group's supervisory college should contribute to effective crisis management planning.

Source: BCBS. 2015. *Progress Report on the Implementation of Principles for Effective Supervisory Colleges*. Basel.

The impact of each failure may not be large, but the chain of failures would have a risk of creating a much larger regional financial crisis.

Central banks provide liquidity to the banking system if the system faces unusual stress and risk of system breakdown. They act as LOLR, providing liquidity to a troubled institution and sustaining its operation to avoid systemic failure. They can provide liquidity without limitation, given their unique ability to create liquid assets in the form of central bank reserves.[78] As banks have inherent instability due to a mismatch in their asset and liability, sudden withdrawals of deposits may trigger an unexpected failure of an even solvent bank. The history of central banking is a history of preventing financial crises by utilizing the power to create unlimited liquidity. They will support banks because a failure may create a larger economic crisis. In principle, liquidity will be provided only to a solvent bank when the bank encounters a liquidity shortage caused by an unexpected system failure or operational mismanagement, but not for insolvency. The liquidity is provided to the extent eligible collaterals are submitted by the bank. However, acting as LOLR is risky because it may not be easy to draw a line between an illiquid and insolvent bank. The amount of liquidity could go beyond the value of the collaterals. In addition, the central bank may need to consider the risk that a banking failure would translate into other bankruptcies and create a much larger impact on the economy. This would create a problem of "too big to fail" and a moral hazard. As LOLR, the central bank needs to make a difficult judgment on whether it would take the risk or not. The judgment inevitably blurs the boundary with the fiscal policy because the illiquid bank may turn into an insolvent bank easily; thus, eventually the loss incurred by the bank may need to be shouldered by taxpayers.

Basically, for liquidity management of cross-border banking, the host central bank has the prime responsibility. The home supervisor can provide liquidity to support the settlement of its own currency, but it is not possible to stop the chain reaction of the failures in other markets. *The Principles for the Supervision of Banks' Foreign Establishments*, or Basel Concordat, stipulates that "the host authority has responsibility for monitoring the liquidity of the foreign bank's establishments in its country… For branches, the initial presumption should be that primary responsibility for supervising liquidity rests with the host authority. Host authorities will often be best equipped to supervise liquidity as it relates to local practices and regulations and the functioning of their domestic money markets… For subsidiaries, primary responsibility for supervising liquidity should rest with the host authority."[79] However, for the host authority, acting as LOLR to a foreign bank has an additional hurdle compared with LOLR to a domestic bank because the central bank may need to consider additional political risk and criticism. As cross-border banking increases, the likelihood of liquidity provision by a host authority will increase. But, given the difficulty involved in the judgment to provide liquidity beyond collateral value as LOLR, it is necessary to realize that the capacity of the host central bank to help foreign banks would practically be limited.

---

[78] BIS. 2014. Re-Thinking the Lender of Last Resort. *BIS Papers*. No.79. Basel.

[79] Basel Committee on Banking Supervision. 1983. *Principles for the Supervision of Banks' Foreign Establishments*. Basel.

The financial shock in March 2020 due to COVID-19 revealed the importance of cross-border arrangements by the central banks, particularly for foreign currency funding. Uncertainty in the markets created a sharp increase in US dollar demand because the US dollar is the international vehicle currency, the medium of exchange for different currencies. The event has shown the importance of a swap line with the US Federal Reserve to provide assurance to the markets. However, this also exhibited a limitation of the swap line for assurance because not all central banks could establish the swap line with the Federal Reserve. it is important to note that the Federal Reserve cannot be the LOLR for all central banks. They have their own policy objectives; thus, they may provide liquidity as long as it will meet their respective policy objective. In other words, given the uncertainty and limitation of LOLR for foreign currencies, the home and host central banks in ASEAN+3 should consider multiple layers of liquidity support and safety nets along with the expansion of cross-border banking and payment services, depending on their size and the potential impacts on payment and settlement systems and regional financial stability. Both central banks should jointly monitor these operations and consider joint liquidity support in case of emergency.

In ASEAN+3, the Chiang Mai Initiative Multilateralization (CMIM) was formed as a network to facilitate multilateral currency swap arrangements for liquidity support among ASEAN+3 member economies, which can request swap transactions of their local currencies with the US dollar or the local currencies of other ASEAN+3 members.[80] The use of CMIM can be considered for a balance-of-payments crisis or the short-term liquidity difficulties of ASEAN+3 member economies due to a macroeconomic shock. However, it is not clear to what extent CMIM can be used for liquidity shortages of financial institutions. CMIM neither targets a country in good economic condition nor a potential negative spillover through a financial network. It was designed to help a temporary liquidity shortage of a member government, not of a financial institution, nor to be acting as LOLR of foreign currency. Thus, home and host central banks in ASEAN+3 must prepare their own cross-border short-term liquidity measures, such as cross-border collateral arrangements and bilateral swap agreements, as additional layers of regional financial safety nets. Desirably, the arrangements can be transformed to provide regional collective liquidity assistance measures during periods of calm.

Cross-border collateral arrangements recognize the home country's government bonds as eligible collateral; thus, by pledging the home country's government bonds to the host central bank, the host central bank can extend a loan to a troubled foreign bank branch. Cross-border repo is similar, but the arrangement is based on a repo transaction. These would prevent a temporary liquidity shortage from developing into default while ensuring the repayment of temporary liquidity to the host central bank. Cross-border collateral arrangements require the expansion of eligible collateral to foreign government bonds. This problem may be considered and solved along with the introduction of "haircuts." It would also require enhancement of cross-border market infrastructures—desirably, system linkages of domestic market infrastructures.[81]

---

[80] An explanation on CMIM can be found in ASEAN+3 Macroeconomic Research Office (AMRO). AMRO and the CMIM. Overview of the CMIM. https://www.amro-asia.org/about-amro/amro-and-the-cmim/.

[81] The Cross-Border Settlement Infrastructure Forum under the Asian Bond Market Initiative proposes Central Securities Depository and Real-Time Gross Settlement linkages to promote the use of cross-border collateral. The recommendations and proposals are described in Asian Development Bank. 2020. *Next Steps for ASEAN+3 Central Securities Depository and Real-Time Gross Settlement Linkages*. Manila.

A bilateral swap agreement can provide local currency liquidity through the host regulator based on the home country's currency. The swap line can be agreed if the home and host countries agree to take the counterparty's country risk. During the COVID-19 crisis, the US dollar swap line offered by the Federal Reserve calmed international markets. The local currency swap lines between ASEAN+3 central banks can alleviate some market stress in the region because a large portion of intraregional transactions are denominated in US dollars but are eventually exchanged for local currencies. However, central banks would need to pay attention to the risk of moral hazard because the home central bank will be taking a risk on behalf of an illiquid bank.

CONCLUSIONS | 5

The COVID-19 crisis has accelerated digital transformation around the world. The use of digital technology has helped governments, businesses, and people manage pandemic responses. E-payments could provide quick, lifesaving financial support directly to people. During the pandemic, various companies and consumers swiftly shifted to e-commerce and food delivery, where online payments are indispensable. In addition, new financing tools, such as crowd finance and online lending based on transactions like accounts receivable and credit scoring from nonfinancial data, have emerged. They provided quick cash to microenterprises and small and medium-sized enterprises to help them survive repeated lockdowns. FinTech will play an even more significant role in recovering from the COVID-19 pandemic.

The progress of financial innovation and digitalization is a great opportunity for the financial industry. Banks have been utilizing financial technologies to improve services (FinTech) and nonfinancial firms have emerged to utilize their technological advantages and offer a part of traditional banking services (TechFin) at a reduced cost, illustrating that the banking industry has increasingly become competitive in recent years.

While being aware of the risks involved, technological innovation in the financial services market should not be fundamentally impeded, and a free and competitive environment should be sufficiently ensured. The measures to be considered in the region include (i) ensuring a level-playing field between existing banks and new entrants; (ii) not granting special treatment in bank licensing standards; (iii) eschewing excessive regulations and supervision; (iv) maintaining the existing entity-based framework in principle, and flexibly and appropriately applying activity- or risk-based regulations and supervision depending on the type of banking service and the extent of influence on financial system and infrastructure; (v) enhancing regulatory and supervisory coordination and cooperation, particularly between home and host authorities; and (vi) adopting and effectively utilizing so-called RegTech for reducing the regulatory burdens of private financial institutions and SupTech for improving the capacity of information sharing among relevant regulators and supervisors. As cybersecurity risks evolve and intensify almost every day and everywhere, further coordination among financial authorities is indispensable, particularly in terms of cross-border data exchanges and standardization.

In the age of digitization, financial transactions will become more globalized as such transactions cross borders more easily. However, cyberspace makes conflicts of geographical as well as functional jurisdictions more complex. Though financial services may go beyond borders, financial regulations continue to be based on territoriality; thus, cross-border regulatory problems must be solved through an appropriate home and host supervisory arrangement. Building trust and confidence in peer regulators is the basis of any effective cross-border regulatory cooperation. Thus, supervisory colleges should be organized for effective coordination among the regulators. To help develop more effective supervisory coordination and cooperation among them, regulators should work more on data standardization and efficient data collection (i.e., RegTech). This will also increase opportunities for the regulators to use advanced technologies in supervision (i.e., SupTech).

Central banks around the world have recognized the importance of cross-border liquidity assistance as one of the lessons from the GFC and the COVID-19 pandemic. Given the uncertainty and limitation of central banks acting as LOLR for foreign currencies, home and host central banks should consider multiple layers of liquidity support and safety nets along with the expansion of cross-border banking and payment services. ASEAN+3 is unique compared with other parts of the world. Intraregional economic linkages are high, like in the EU. But the member economies have their own currencies, and they are in different stages of economic development, though the differences can be narrowed rapidly. The region is leading the worldwide transformation of digital financial services; hence, the opportunities as well as risks involved may be high. Home and host central banks in ASEAN+3 must prepare their own cross-border, short-term liquidity measures, such as cross-border collateral arrangements and bilateral swap agreements, as another layer of regional financial safety nets. It is important to consider regional risk mitigation measures along with the rapid expansion of new financial services before any crisis happens.

REFERENCES

ASEAN+3 Macroeconomic Research Office (AMRO). AMRO and the CMIM. Overview of the CMIM. https://www.amro-asia.org/about-amro/amro-and-the-cmim/.

Asian Development Bank. 2020. *Next Steps for ASEAN+3 Central Securities Depository and Real-Time Gross Settlement Linkages: A Progress Report of the Cross-Border Settlement Infrastructure Forum.* Manila. https://dx.doi.org/10.22617/TCS200193-2.

—————. 2021a. *Asian Development Outlook 2021: Financing a Green and Inclusive Recovery.* https://dx.doi.org/10.22617/FLS210163-3.

—————. 2021b. *Harnessing Digitization for Remittances in Asia and the Pacific.* https://dx.doi.org/10.22617/TCS210263-2.

Amann, D. M. ed. 2014. Jurisdictional, Preliminary, and Procedural Concerns. In *Benchbook on International Law.* American Society of International Law. https://www.asil.org/sites/default/files/benchbook/ASIL_Benchbook_Complete.pdf.

Association of Southeast Asian Nations (ASEAN). 2021. Payment Systems in the Digital Age: Case of ASEAN. *ASEAN Policy Brief.* No. 4. https://asean.org/wp-content/uploads/2021/09/ASEAN-Policy-Brief-4_FINAL-06Apr2021-1.pdf.

BaFin Passporting. European Passports. https://www.bafin.de/EN/Aufsicht/BankenFinanzdienstleister/Passporting/passporting_artikel_en.html.

Banchongduang, S. 2021. PromptPay Now Linked to DuitNow. *Bangkok Post.* 19 June. https://www.bangkokpost.com/business/2134811/promptpay-now-linked-to-duitnow.

Bank for International Settlements (BIS) 2014. Re-thinking the Lender of Last Resort. *BIS Papers.* No.79. Basel. https://www.bis.org/publ/bppdf/bispap79.htm.

—————. 2017. Designing Frameworks for Central Bank Liquidity Assistance: Addressing New Challenges. *Committee on the Global Financial System Papers.* No. 58. https://www.bis.org/publ/cgfs58.htm.

—————. 2019a. *Sound Practices: Implications of Fintech Developments for Banks and Bank Supervisors.* Basel Committee on Banking Supervision. https://www.bis.org/bcbs/publ/d431.pdf.

—————. 2019b. *Report on Open Banking and Application Programming Interfaces (APIs).* https://www.bis.org/bcbs/publ/d486.htm.

Basel Committee on Banking Supervision. 1975. *Report on the Supervision of Banks' Foreign Establishments.* https://www.bis.org/publ/bcbs00a.pdf.

————. 1983. *Principles for the Supervision of Banks' Foreign Establishments*. Basel

————. 1992. *Minimum Standards for the Supervision of International Banking Groups and Their Cross-Border Establishments*. https://www.bis.org/publ/bcbsc314.htm.

————. 1996. *The Supervision of Cross-Border Banking*. Basel.

————. 2003. *Management and Supervision of Cross-Border Electronic Banking Activities*. Basel.

————. 2010a. *Good Practice Principles on Supervisory Colleges*. Basel.

————. 2010b. *Good Practice Principles on Supervisory Colleges*. Basel.

————. 2015. *Progress Report on the Implementation of Principles for Effective Supervisory Colleges*. Basel.

Boar, C. and R. Szemere. Payments Go (Even More) Digital. *Bank for International Settlements* (BIS). Payment Statistics. https://www.bis.org/statistics/payment_stats/commentary2011.htm.

Bucak, S. 2021. French Neobanks Try to Keep It Simple as They Grow Quickly. *Financial Times*. 24 January. https://www.ft.com/content/881bd0a6-96de-4776-818f-f81f2e0230f5.

Calvo, D. et al. 2018. Financial Supervisory Architecture: What Has Changed after the Crisis? *FSI Insights on Policy Implementation*. No. 8. Basel.

Cambridge Centre for Alternative Finance, Asian Development Bank Institute, and FinTechSpace. 2019. *ASEAN FinTech Ecosystem Benchmarking Study*. https://www.jbs.cam.ac.uk/wp-content/uploads/2020/08/2019-ccaf-asean-fintech-ecosystem-benchmarking-study.pdf; https://www.jbs.cam.ac.uk/faculty-research/centres/alternative-finance/publications/the-asean-fintech-ecosystem-benchmarking-study/.

Crisanto, J. C., J. Ehrentraud, and M. Fabian. 2021. Big Techs in Finance: Regulatory Approaches and Policy Options. *FSI Briefs* No. 12. March. https://www.bis.org/fsi/fsibriefs12.pdf.

Deloitte. 2019. *Robots are Here: The Rise of Robo-Advisers in Asia Pacific*. https://www2.deloitte.com/content/dam/Deloitte/sg/Documents/financial-services/sea-fsi-robo-advisers-asia-pacific.pdf.

Deloitte Center for Financial Services. 2018. *2019 Banking and Capital Markets Outlook Reimagining Transformation*. September. https://www2.deloitte.com/content/dam/Deloitte/us/Documents/financial-services/us-fsi-dcfs-2019-banking-cap-markets-outlook.pdf.

————. 2019. *2020 Banking and Capital Markets Outlook: Fortifying the Core for the Next Wave of Disruption*. December. https://www2.deloitte.com/content/dam/Deloitte/lu/Documents/financial-services/lu-2020-banking-and-capital-markets-outlook.pdf.

Ehrentraud, J., D. G. Ocampo, and C. Q. Vega. 2020. Regulating FinTech Financing: Digital Banks and FinTech Platforms. *FSI Insights* No. 27. BIS. 27 August. https://www.bis.org/fsi/publ/insights27.htm.

Ehrentraud, J. et al. 2020. Policy Responses to Fintech: A Cross-Country Overview. *FSI Insights on Policy Implementation* No. 23. BIS. https://www.bis.org/fsi/publ/insights23.pdf.

Escobar, S. 2022. Coinbase Launches Cryptocurrency Remittance Pilot Program in Mexico. *Barron's*. 15 February. https://www.barrons.com/articles/coinbase-cryptocurrency-remittance-pilot-program-mexico-51644952896.

European Banking Authority. Credit Institutions Register. https://euclid.eba.europa.eu/register/cir/search.

European Central Bank. 2017. *Guide to Assignments of Fintech Credit Institution License Applications*. Frankfurt.

Ernst & Young. 2020. *UK FinTech: Moving Mountains and Moving Mainstream*. https://assets.ey.com/content/dam/ey-sites/ey-com/en_gl/topics/emeia-financial-services/ey-uk-fintech-2020-report.pdf.

Financial Action Task Force. 2021. *Cross-Border Payments Survey Results on Implementation of the FATF Standards*. https://www.fatf-gafi.org/publications/fatfrecommendations/documents/cross-border-payments.html.

Financial Services Sector Coordinating Council. https://fsscc.org/about-fsscc/.

Fintech News. 2021. Instant Cross-Border Payments Will Soon Become a Reality in APAC. 30 November. https://fintechnews.sg/57596/payments/instant-cross-border-payments-will-soon-become-a-reality-in-apac/.

Financial Stability Board. 2011. *Shadow Banking: Strengthening Oversight and Regulation*. October.

—————. 2017. *Summary Report on Financial Sector Cybersecurity Regulations, Guidance and Supervisory Practices*. Basel.

—————. 2019. *Fintech and Market Structure in Financial Services: Market Developments and Potential Financial Stability Implications*. https://www.fsb.org/wp-content/uploads/P140219.pdf.

—————. 2020. *FSB Report on Market Fragmentation*. Basel.

FSC Korea. 2021. "Toss Bank (3rd Internet-only bank) Approved for Banking Business." (unofficial translation). 9 June.

Ghosh, P. 2021. 3 Major Banks Plan More Branch Closings As Thousands Shutter—In U.S. And U.K.—Amid Covid, Digital Growth. *Forbes*. 23 April. https://www.forbes.com/sites/palashghosh/2021/04/23/3-major-banks-plan-more-branch-closings-as-thousands-shutter-in-us-and-uk-amid-covid-digital-growth/?sh=17276f465bc6.

Insider Intelligence. 2022. What Neobanks Are, How They Work and the Top Neobanks in the US & World in 2022. 9 January. https://www.insiderintelligence.com/insights/neobanks-explained-list.

InsightsArtist. 2021. 2021 Global Fintech Rankings. December. https://insightsartist.com/2021-global-fintech-rankings/#:~:text=The%20USA%20tops%20the%20Global,the%20same%20period%20last%20year.

Institute of International Finance. 2019. *Addressing Market Fragmentation: The Need for Enhanced Global Regulatory Cooperation*. Washington, DC. January. https://www.iif.com/portals/0/Files/IIF%20FSB%20Fragmentation%20Report.pdf.

IOSCO. 2015. *IOSCO Task Force on Cross-Border Regulation Final Report*. September. https://www.iosco.org/library/pubdocs/pdf/IOSCOPD507.pdf.

KPMG International. 2022. *Pulse of Fintech H2'21*. January. https://home.kpmg/xx/en/home/insights/2022/01/pulse-of-fintech-h2-2021-global.html.

Monetary Authority of Singapore. 2021. Singapore and Thailand Launch World's First Linkage of Real-time Payment Systems. 29 April. https://www.mas.gov.sg/news/media-releases/2021/singapore-and-thailand-launch-worlds-first-linkage-of-real-time-payment-systems.

N26. 2021. N26 Exceeds 2 Million Customers in France in 4 Years. 10 June. https://n26.com/en-fr/press/press-release/n26-exceeds-2-million-customers-in-france-in-4-years.

Nicoli, M. and U. Ahmed. 2019. World Bank Blogs. "How Digital Remittances Can Help Drive Sustainable Development." https://blogs.worldbank.org/psd/how-digital-remittances-can-help-drive-sustainable-development.

Organisation for Economic Co-operation and Development. 2020. *Digital Disruption in Banking and its Impact on Competition*. https://www.oecd.org/competition/digital-disruption-in-banking-and-its-impact-on-competition-2020.pdf.

PYMNTS. 2021a. Revolut Bank Granted Full EU Banking License Amid Criticisms of Unfair Competition. 20 December. https://www.pymnts.com/digital-first-banking/2021/revolut-bank-granted-full-european-union-banking-license-amid-criticisms-unfair-competition.

PYMNTS and Stellar Development Foundation. 2021b. *The Digital Currency Shift: The Cross-Border Remittances Report*. September. https://www.pymnts.com/wp-content/uploads/2021/09/PYMNTS-Cross-Border-Remittances-Report-September-2021.pdf.

ResearchDive. 2022. *Robo Advisory Market Report*. https://www.researchdive.com/8537/robo-advisory-market.

Restoy, F. 2021. FinTech Regulation: How to Achieve a Level Playing Field. *FSI Occasional Papers* No. 17. Bank for International Settlements. 2 February. https://www.bis.org/fsi/fsipapers17.htm.

Revolut. 2022. Revolut Launches as a Bank in 10 Western European Markets, Now Available in 28 Countries. 11 January. https://www.revolut.com/news/revolut_launches_as_a_bank_in_10_western_european_markets_now_available_in_28_countries.

Seeh, F. 2021. How New Entrants Are Redefining Cross-Border Payments. *Ernst & Young*. 23 February. https://www.ey.com/en_gl/banking-capital-markets/how-new-entrants-are-redefining-cross-border-payments.

Srinivas, V. and A. Ross. 2018. Accelerating Digital Transformation in Banking: Findings from the Global Consumer Survey on Digital Banking. *Deloitte Insights*. 9 October. https://www2.deloitte.com/us/en/insights/industry/financial-services/digital-transformation-in-banking-global-customer-survey.html.

Statista. Digital Remittances—Worldwide. https://www.statista.com/outlook/dmo/fintech/digital-payments/digital-remittances/worldwide (accessed 12 September 2022).

————. Number of Active Online Banking Users Worldwide in 2020 with Forecasts from 2021 to 2024, by Region. https://www.statista.com/statistics/1228757/online-banking-users-worldwide/ (accessed 12 September 2022).

————. Robo-Advisors—Worldwide. https://www.statista.com/outlook/dmo/fintech/digital-investment/robo-advisors/worldwide?currency=usd (accessed 12 September 2022).

————. Value of Assets under Management of Selected Robo-Advisors Worldwide as of March 2022. https://www.statista.com/statistics/573291/aum-of-selected-robo-advisors-globally/ (accessed 12 September 2022).

UK Finance. 2016. What is Passporting and Why Does it Matter? *Brexit Quick Brief* No. 3. https://www.ukfinance.org.uk/sites/default/files/uploads/pdf/BQB3-What-is-passporting-and-why-does-it-matter-UKF.pdf.

Visa Economic Empowerment Institute. 2021. *The Rise of Digital Remittances: How Innovation Is Improving Global Money Movement.* https://usa.visa.com/content/dam/VCOM/global/ms/documents/veei-the-rise-of-digital-remittances.pdf.

Walsh, D. 2021. Paying with Bitcoin: These Are the Major Companies That Accept Crypto as Payment. *EuroNews Next.* 4 December. https://www.euronews.com/next/2022/11/30/record-inflation-which-country-in-europe-has-been-worst-hit-and-how-do-they-compare.

Webber, D. 2021. Cryptocurrency in Cross-Border Payments: After Coinbase's Success, Can Crypto Flourish beyond Assets? *Forbes.* 21 April. https://www.forbes.com/sites/danielwebber/2021/04/21/cryptocurrency-in-cross-border-payments-after-coinbases-success-can-crypto-flourish-beyond-assets/?sh=6bd2e8d6416f.

World Bank. Data. Commercial Bank Branches (Per 100,000 Adults)—Indonesia, Malaysia, Korea, Rep., Singapore, Thailand. https://data.worldbank.org/indicator/FB.CBK.BRCH.P5?locations=ID-MY-KR-SG-TH (accessed 12 September 2022).

WorldPay. 2022. *The Global Payments Report.* https://worldpay.globalpaymentsreport.com/en.

Ziegler, T. et al. 2021. *The 2nd Global Alternative Finance Market Benchmarking Report.* Cambridge Centre for Alternative Finance. June. https://www.jbs.cam.ac.uk/faculty-research/centres/alternative-finance/publications/the-2nd-global-alternative-finance-market-benchmarking-report/.

www.ingramcontent.com/pod-product-compliance
Lightning Source LLC
Chambersburg PA
CBHW042034220326
41599CB00045BA/7392